A MULTI-THEMATIC ANALYSIS OF CONVENTIONS AND CONTEMPORANEITY IN THE HIMALAYAS AS DEPICTED IN SR HARNOT'S CATS TALK

A MULTI-THEMATIC ANALYSIS OF CONVENTIONS AND CONTEMPORANEITY IN THE HIMALAYAS AS DEPICTED IN SR HARNOT'S CATS TALK

Abhyudita Gautam

AUTHORSPRESS

Worldwide Circulation through Authorspress Global Network

First Published in 2023

by

Authorspress

Q-2A Hauz Khas Enclave, New Delhi-110 016 (India)

Phone: (0) 9818049852

E-mail: authorspressgroup@gmail.com

Website: www.authorspressbooks.com

A Multi-Thematic Analysis of Conventions and Contemporaneity in the Himalayas as Depicted in SR Harnot's *Cats Talk*

ISBN 978-93-5529-575-0

Printed in India at Thomson Press (India) Limited

Contents

Introduction

This book is an attempt to deeply delve into the concerns with modernity sneaking into the pristine environs of the hills and how the inhabitants have reacted to the advent of new modes in socio-cultural spheres. However, the objective of the research would also be to assess the negative and positive impacts of this remodeled, remolded, and refashioned society on the old people, environment, caste politics, religious faith, and the women of the hills. It is based on the stories that attempt at establishing the changes in the modern world that had remained alien to the people of the hills for a long but due to developmental activity and technological advancement, globalisation has slowly seeped into a new-paced society. The book is an attempt to analyse the effects of these changes and how they have been adapted very well by the people but how they have made sure that the traditions of the old culture are retained in a better version which makes them more relevant to be followed.

The objectives of the analysis contained in this book are:

- To elucidate how women have challenged the patriarchal customs of society
- To evaluate the impact of environmental changes that have led to degradation and how people resort to traditional ways to conserve it.
- To indicate how the educated subalterns resist subjugation
- To analyse the loneliness of the left-behind parents
- To delve into the concept of faith in the deities of the hills

The questions that the analysis aims to answer are: –

- How have the left behind, empty-nest elderly aged parents of the out-migrated children, adjusted to the lonely life in the hills?
- How have the women rejected the social norms to become self-reliant and learned to ignore the social taboos, liberating themselves?

- How has education helped the subalterns to understand the dynamics of the casteist milieu of the society and encouraged them to deconstruct the hierarchy by manipulating the rules of casteism, utilising their status for their welfare?
- Has the cultural heritage been disturbed by modern lifestyles or people have still managed to keep them alive simultaneously?

The analysis would be relevant for scholars who are looking at the sociological changes that are creeping into society with the introduction of the new ultra-modern technology. The majority of the people of the state belong to rural areas and continue with the traditional ways of living. However, with the spread of education, with the opening of educational institutes in every nook and corner of the area, they are exposed to the western and urban culture through modern gazettes and the internet. Due to the mountainous terrain, the people cannot travel to the urban areas frequently which keeps them connected to their traditional ways of living.

CHAPTER 1

SR Harnot

S. R. Harnot is an eminent fiction writer who has carved a niche for himself in the world of Hindi short story writing. Apart from writing about the lives in the majestic mountains, and babbling rivers, his stories focus on the complexities and dilemmas faced by the simple folk of the hills due to the changing social setup. With his curious eyes, he keenly observes and minutely describes the deeply rooted social, cultural, and religious pattern of the Pahari society, which creates a world that is not caged in time. In this regard, his stories have often been placed in the storytelling tradition of Premchand. Harnot skillfully merges the complexities of life and subtly captures the flow of life in a style that makes them look authentic. His short stories present the little joys and unceasing ironies in the life of the Pahari people. His narratives explore the arising from the interference of political crooks and religious hypocrites, class and caste discriminations, his stories focus on human relationships. While the mountains, forests, water, land, flora, and fauna of the Himalayas are present as backdrop melodies, his stories focus on the issues of women, caste, class, nature, ecology, democracy, and development. Within the framework of Pahari culture, Harnot weaves the changing truths of contemporary times. On the one side, he is disturbed by the erosion of his culture; on the other, he creates characters who strive to realise their full humanity.

Harnot writes in simple and lucid language that is infused with the aroma of the indigenousness of the Pahari vicinity could be seen in the language of his stories. The local words and phrases prevalent in the mountains of Himachal provide a special colour to the language in his stories. The events in his stories are almost cinematic and nature's vignettes draw on the painter's palette. However, it is in the delineation of character that Harnot displays mastery. The rich layering of the text, matched with the simplicity of narration makes his stories a delight as well as a challenge for the translators. His short stories have been translated into various languages, including English.

Successful translations of Harnot's short stories have already been published to an eager response.

Awards Won by the Author

SR Harnot has been a recipient of many awards and honours. He has been awarded the International Indu Sharma Katha Samman (awarded in London) and Himachal State Academy Award in 2007 for the book *Daarosh and Other Stories*, Pakhi and JC Joshi word seeker popular writer award by the Independent Media Initiative Society, Delhi for the year 2009 for the collection 'Jeenkathi Aur Kahaniyan', Jagdish Chandra Smriti Samman for the year 2012 for the collection of stories named 'Mitti Ke Log', "Tourism and Literature Award-2009" by Himachal Tourism Development Corporation for outstanding contribution in the field of tourism and literature. Distinguished Literary Award by Creative News Foundation, Delhi, All India Bharatendu Harishchandra Award, Himachal Kesari Award, Best Literary Award by the Center of Ancient Arts, Chandigarh, 'Hindi Seva Samman' of 2010 by Malwa Theater Committee, and Kritika Communication Mumbai. He also received the Fiction Writer of the Year Award 2019 by Daily Newspaper. Divya Himachal conferred the Excellence Award 2019 for overall literary contribution to the writer.

His stories have been prescribed in various university courses like the story "Maa" which is taught in the MA Part-II syllabus at the University of Kerala and "m.com" which is included in the higher secondary curriculum of the Department of Education, Government of Kerala. The English translation of "Lal Hota Drakht" in the Ph.D. English syllabus of Central University of Himachal Pradesh, Dharamshala, and B.A.Part-II of Himachal Pradesh University as "The Reddening Tree", the Story "Chashmidid" included is in the syllabus of B.A. in Gautam Buddha University, Noida, Selection of the story "Abhi" at Jain University, Bangalore (Karnataka) in a Hindi course for 2016-2019 specially designed for B.Com, B.Sc, and BBM students and published by Oxford University Press. The curriculum is designed for 7th and 8th-grade Vibhav Hindi Pathmala including Kahani "Maa Reads", and Story "Stone Games" at the Central University of Punjab.

Stories in the Book *Cats Talk*

The book titled *Cats Talk* is published by Cambridge Scholars Publishing is an anthology of translated stories in English, edited by

Khemraj Sharma and Meenakshi F. Paul that have touched many themes in the lives of the people of this state, residing in the hills who have maintained the old lifestyles that seem to have been frozen over time and yet melting away slowly due to the heat of changes that have been brought about. They may no longer live in a cocoon and are exposed to a more realistic and materialistic world. There are twelve stories in the book that cover many aspects of the lives of the people of the hills. There are empty-nest syndrome, casteism, feminism, subjugation, rebellion, isolation, alienation, migration, exploitation, environmental issues, and commercialisation that has been represented in the stories and some of them like "Slur" and "The River Has Vanished" have dealt with two issues in one story.

"Cats Talk" was originally published in Hindi as "Billiyan Batiyati Hain" in the collection, *Daarosh Tatha Anya Kahaniyan* and has been translated into English by R. K. Shukla and Manjari Tiwari. The story first appeared in the Hindi magazine *Pahal* in 1995; its English translation was published in the Journal, 'Of Indian Literature' in 2013. It has even been staged as a play by the students in H.P. Youth Festival. The story depicts the harsh reality of migration from villages and its impact on people. It is the story of an old alienated and left-back mother who has been facing the challenges posed by the hawks of society who are eyeing her property. She finds solace in the pet animals that she has reared including a cat who accompanies her all the time from kitchen to bedroom almost taking the place of her child. The neighbours and relatives of the village have also been very helpful towards Amma who has developed a bond with them. The last part of the story describes the repentance of the son who had by now realised that the cat was luckier than him to have received the motherly love that he longed for instead of the money that he had come to borrow from his mother.

"The Twenty-Foot Bapu Ji", "Bees Foot Ke Bapu Ji", is also part of *Daarosh Tatha Anya Kahaniyan* translated by Meenakshi F. Paul and Khem Raj Sharma. The story talks about the changing father-son relationship. Harnot skillfully juxtaposes the statue of Mahatma Gandhi with the life of old Chachu to portray the abandoning of old values by the younger generation and the compulsions of the economy and social prestige. This abandonment of values is paralleled by the retreat of Chachu from his son's life, which in turn is reflected by the elevation of Gandhi's statue from six feet to twenty feet which was an oxymoron as the morals and principles had been disgraced and let down with the raising of the statue.

"The Reddening Tree" was first published as "Lal Hota Darakht" in the anthology *Akashbel* (1988). Harnot modified the story and included it in *Daarosh Tatha Anya Kahaniyan* (2001). The story has been translated into English by Meenakshi F. Paul. It is a powerful and moving story, narrated in almost lyrical terms, about a poor farmer, torn between his religious obligations and his means, and his land and the marriage of his daughter, mortgaging his land for the wedding ceremony and finally the innocence of the daughter who found a solution to the problem which leaves the readers awestruck. The eco-feministic theory is quite apparent in the story. The story is featured in the anthology of translated work, *Short Stories of Himachal Pradesh.*

"Daarosh" is a fine and subtle delineation of a typical custom of a tribal area in Himachal Pradesh. It first appeared with the same title in the Hindi magazine *Hans* in 1997 and was then published in *Daarosh Tatha Anya Kahaniyan.* The story has been translated into English by Khem Raj Sharma. Daarosh means 'by force'. An old age dying custom of that particular area is called 'Daarosh dublub' meaning forcible marriage. The story revolves around an educated village girl who is asserting her resistance against the disempowering patriarchal setup of her society very strongly. The story captures the complexities that arise when modern civilisation penetrates the fortified society. Though being an upholder of perseverance of the rich culture, Harnot is also known for voicing his criticism against the social evils in the name of customs and traditions. The role of education and modernity would be analysed in detail in this story.

"The Saddle" was originally published in Hindi as "Jinkathi" in a literary magazine. The story brings out the intricacies of the 'Bhunda', an ancient and terrifying Himachal festival involving human sacrifice, and how the Dalit is transformed into a Brahmin to be used as a scapegoat for the sacrifice. The chosen man, however, bargains for a better deal for his community that the politicians present had to agree upon in the presence of hundreds of people who had gathered to witness the event. The ability of a poor man to transform this religious ceremony into an opportunity is a rebellion against the long-standing conventions of making the unprivileged as an object of sacrifice. The story, "m.com" was published as 'Em Dot Com" (2001) and has been translated into English by Meenakshi

F. Paul. The story is a powerful story about the ironies that arise with economic development and modern technology in traditional societies and how the old mother is unable to comprehend the modern ways of registering her cattle in the software through the computer when she is caught in a situation where no one could help her.

"Ma Reads" was first published as "Ma Padhti Hai" in the leading Hindi magazine *Hans.* It has been translated into English by Ira Raja. It is the story of a writer and his hardworking independent mother. Her son is an acknowledged writer in the city but his illiterate mother back home is unaware of his literary achievements. However, he is quite surprised to know that she has been reading all of his stories all these years.

"Savarna Devta, Dalit Devta" was published in Hindi with the same title in the collection of short stories and has been translated into English by R. K. Shukla and Manjari Tiwari. It records the pain and anguish of a Dalit boy, who could not reconcile himself to being subjugated and mistreated based on caste. The inhumanity of the practice of caste pollution perturbs him greatly. He challenges the religious conventions that lead to the isolation of people who are lower down in the caste hierarchy and concludes that they are a part of the conspiracy to keep them permanently in a specific position.

"Slur" was published as "Kaalikh" in the monthly journal *Himprasth.* It was later included in *Jinkathi Aur Anya Kahaniyan* and has been translated into English by Khem Raj Sharma and Meenakshi F. Paul. It is the story of a bold young Dalit widow, Shyama, who has a son born a couple of years after the death of her husband. Her husband had died of insanity caused by his indulgence in witchcraft and thereafter Shyama has managed on her own. In a conspiracy to deny her and her son their rightful share of her husband's property and to prevent her son from being educated, she is rebuked and insulted by the very men who had exploited her physically and financially. Instead of being dominated this time for the right of her son, she exposes their hypocrisy and shames them before the whole village council.

"In the Name of Gods" was first published in *Pahal* in 2006 with the title "Devataon Ke Bahane". It is the story of Som, an educated Dalit boy, who wants to eradicate the backwardness of his area. He devises a plan and executes it in an intelligent way that would ensure that development finally comes to his area. Som finally emerges as the leader of the village and is acknowledged by everyone. "The River Has Vanished", originally written as "Nadi Ghayab Hai", was published in the short story collection *Mitti Ke Log*. It has been translated into English by Ravi Nandan Sinha and is part of his anthology of translations, *Great Hindi Short Stories*. A book on Harnot's environment-based stories has also been edited in Hindi by Usha Rani Rao with the Hindi title (2018). In this story, Harnot exhibits his engagement with environmental issues and promotes the idea of development with conservation. In Himachal, as in all of India, rivers are worshipped and have mythological legends attached to them. In this story, Teekam, a village lad understands the deep conspiracy of the rich and the powerful to tame the river to gain profits, not caring about the villagers who would be deprived of their livelihoods and transforming the whole land into a barren place. He intelligently uses the religious sentiments of the people in the village Devta to prevent the construction of a dam on the river. The Devta is shown to have revenged through the villagers.

'Aabhi' is taken from Harnot's latest short story collection *Lytton Block Gir Raha Hai* (2014) and has been translated by Meenakshi F. Paul. It is the story of a bird, locally called Aabhi. Legend has it that the bird keeps the lake by the name of Serolsar in the Kullu district of Himachal Pradesh clean by not allowing even a twig to float on the pure and placid lake waters. In this age of environmental degradation and exploitation of natural resources, the bird becomes a living symbol of natural coexistence. Aabhi and the Mother Snake Goddess, live together in a temple nearby in harmony which is quintessential of the people living in the hills and how the wildlife is conserved by the demons in human form.

CHAPTER 2

Translation and Short Stories

Cats Talk is an anthology of translated stories that were originally penned down in Hindi by the author and had later been translated into English. Flavours of the regional dialects are clearly visible in the translated versions, besides the cultural dispositions that remain intact in the stories enliven the narration. To understand the dynamics of translation, it is important to delve into the intricacies of the process of conversion and adaption from one language to the other. A branch of discipline has emerged that exclusively deals with the theory and practical implementation for this exercise.

Translation Studies

Before analysing the translated stories in their true essence, the concept and the dynamics of translation need to be elaborated upon to be able to comprehend how the translated works do justice to the original stories. The very meaning of the word translation is to carry the thoughts and ideas expressed in one language to another language so that the readership of a particular text is widened reaching a larger number of people. According to the Cambridge Dictionary, translation is an activity or process of changing the words of one language into the words of another language, which have the same meaning. Further, it can be added that translation is the communication of the meaning of a text in a source language into a comprehensive version of the target language without causing any loss to the original message. The purpose of translation is to enrich and expand the literature of both the source and the target language.

The activity of translation can be dated back to 3000B.C. which can be attributed to the bilingual inscriptions found in the Sphinx from the ancient Egyptian kingdom. In the later years, with trade relations being established between different civilisations, we can find more of Greco-Egyptian translations. However, it was the translation of the Holy Bible from Greek to English and further into various languages of different countries of the world that enhanced the activity of translation like never before, bringing the religious aspect into the translation business. Such was the impact of the translated Bibles by the Christian Missionaries that now it is even being translated into Tribal languages. As Derrida says "The best translation resembles this royal cape. It remains separate from the body to which it is nevertheless conjoined, wedding it, not wedded to it" (Derrida 194)

Further coming to modern English Literature and the translated works in English Literature, the works of Michel Foucault and Jacques Derrida, whose critical essays form the important pillars of critical theories in English Literature, had been translated from French to English. We can say that now most of the literature of the world from all four genres has been translated into English which has widened the scope of research and bridged the gap between the native and the mainstream literature of the world. Talking about India, we all know how diverse and rich is the lingual legacy and heritage of the Indian languages. In India, the first translation is believed to be that of the Kalidasa which was translated from the scholarly Sanskrit to the common man's Prakrit language, which was known as 'Chhaya' which is a Hindi word that means Shadow or to be more precise a reflection.

Talking of Translations in English, the colonial past cannot be ignored and we can say that it was the British who translated most of the works written i.e., Vernacular Hindi to that of English, to have a better glimpse and understanding of the Indian socio-cultural values and lifestyles. They translated the Hindu scriptures into English which was a way to comprehend and understand the Indian faith system and religious affiliation. In 1789, the first Indian Drama, *Abhigyan Shakuntlam* written by Kalidasa, was translated from Sanskrit into English as *Sacontla (1789)* by Sir Willaim Jones. It was later translated into forty-six languages. People seemed to be interested in reading M.K. Gandhi's writings as well which were also translated into English. Gandhi translated many of his texts into English and got them published in the South African journal *Indian Opinion*. Another important essay that he had written in Gujarati and translated into English was *Hind Swaraj*. Tagore's *Gitanjali* was a collection of Bengali poems that were translated by Tagore himself into English in 1912 as *Gitanjali: Song Offerings* with a Preface by William Butler Yeats.

Coming to the writers of Himachal Pradesh, much of the literature written here is written in Hindi and Pahari dialects which are written in the Devnagri Script. However, not many of the works of the writers from Himachal Pradesh have been translated into English.SR Harnot is one such writer who has written many stories in Hindi, out of which twelve have been translated into English by various translators and these have been compiled into a book edited by Khemraj Sharma and Meenakshi F. Paul called *Cats Talk* published in 2018. Translating these stories into English has broadened its scope for research as well as comparison with the literature of other regions and writers. Whether to translate a native language into English, one has to understand the postcolonial spaces and times. Even today, many countries including India face the problem of adorning a national identity in a multilingual state. The literary studies in these nations therefore often center around one link language that would be suitable for all. In India, there has to be one language that would voice the experiences and history of the Indian populace. English enables writers, scholars, critics, and ordinary Indian readers to access the regional literature and connect between the literature of the different languages.

The importance of translating the regional and Hindi works into English becomes more relevant as more and more Indian and foreign scholars are showing interest in exploring the cultures of the various regions that are vividly portrayed in these natives' literature. States like Himachal Pradesh which don't have a specific language system, with a script, rely on Hindi as a medium of expression, making the literature richer by adding flavours and aroma to the fictional documentation of the cultures in various genres. Talking about contemporary approaches like Cultural Studies and Post-Colonial approaches to translation, translation is viewed as an ideological activity that can be understood in its social, cultural, and historical context. The traditional theory of Translation emphasises the importance of translating the essence and not just the words into the other language. The traditional theory also believes that translated work is inferior and secondary to the original work. This concept however is rejected by the contemporary theory which focuses on the fact that translation can be understood only by its cultural and historical context.

The translation of Hindi texts into English has yet to expand to other nations and foreign publishers. Most of the translation of

Hindi into English is done by Indian translators and published by Indian publishers. According to Nicola Pozza, in his essay "Translating from Indian and the moving space of Translation" published in *India in Translation Through Hindi Literature: A Plurality of Voices (2010),* the colonial language is considered to be beneficial for promoting Hindi Literature in India to other non-Hindi speaking states. Out of the total translations from Hindi to English, 25% have been translated to English, 10% to Oriya, and 7% to German and Bengali each. Translation of the text into English would prove to be a boon for the writers as their books and the culture that they have depicted in their writings can be accessed by people from the western world. To unravel the mystery of the culture and livelihood of the Indian subcontinent, the readers of the western world would delve deep into these translated texts. As observed by D.N. Devy in the following lines:

> English has been the socially privileging language in India for over a century, and the importance of English in trade and technology makes it the most attractive choice as the medium of school education. Invariably, therefore, the children sent to English medium schools need to be instructed in Indian myths, epics, and other narratives in English translation. The translation is now the bridge between the literature of the past and the present generation. It has also become the bridge between new writings in Indian languages and the new leadership that is gradually losing touch with these languages. (Devy 123)

Therefore, it becomes necessary that the Hindi texts be converted to English and other European languages so that the cultural studies of a particular country or province in India, reach a wider readership that would enhance the literary, racial, folk, and ethnical understanding of a particular region. Talking of Himachal Pradesh, Harnot has emerged as a writer whose writings have been ingrained completely in the social fabric of the state. His writings are worthy of translations as they do justice by presenting the authentic flavours of the state and its people in a socio-political context and also covering the contemporary issue of the environment. This has been explained in the following lines:

> Harish Trivedi notes the euphoria around Translation Studies and their growth in the world and contends that by popular perceptions Translation Studies "never had it so good". Many works of our regional writers are getting translated and the diasporic phenomenon of cultural translation has put the spotlight back on us. We are, it seems, moving towards a translated world, a global cultural village; or as Benjamin wistfully wondered about in "The Task of the Translator", the

> establishment of a "pure language" with translation bridging gaps between languages and thereby, cultures. (Patra 68)

According to Khemraj and Meenakshi F. Paul in the Introduction to the book *Cats Talk*, translating the stories of SR Harnot has been challenging as he is recognised as a writer who reveals the true essence of society, exposing the darker side too in an inimitable way. Words from the local dialect have been used by the writer in the Hindi stories and have been added in the translated works as well. The editors elaborate:

> The rich layers of meaning conveyed through a straightforward narrative technique in Harnot pose a delightful challenge for the translators. Local words and syntactical patterns apart, the anachronistic but lived culture of his world together with the deep ingress of the present times into it, test the translators' agility. An adequate translation of many of his stories cannot be wrought without the translators immersing themselves in the complex cultural matrix of his society. Thus, while his characters are universally human, the field of their humanity is particularly specific. This is reflected in the many translations of his texts, which range from close translations, adaptations, and transcreations to inter-semiotic migrations. The various translators in this collection have naturally interpreted the stories severally and translated them according to their diverse translating practice and belief. Hence, there are varying spellings of Hindi and Pahari words in different stories. (Sharma et al 3)

They have further also pointed out the words from the local language that have been used in the texts and not translated into the English language to keep the flavours of the culture intact in the stories. They quoted the words that have been used from the local languages in the "Introduction" to *Cats Talk*. For e.g., words like devtas',' 'goor' and 'bidi'. However, they have also changed the 'chariot/palanquin' for the 'rath' (open palanquin with a canopy) of the devata and the priest/oracle/vehicle for the devata's 'gur'. In our view, these variations add to the richness of the narratives and the reader's holistic reading experience by adding different strokes of nuance and texture. While striving for the desired balance between the two languages, the translators have almost always given primacy to the original. For example, relational names have been mostly retained, 'Amma' (mother), 'Baba/Bapu/Pita' (father, grandfather, respectful term for an old man), 'Chachu/Kaka' (father's younger brother, respectful term for an older man), 'Chhote Pita' (father's younger brother), 'Badi Ma' (wife of father's older brother). Even so, they have not shied from accepting precedents set by earlier translators that aid fluency, such as following the English rule for making plurals. In Hindi and Pahari, plurals may be synonymous with the singular, e.g., 'neta' (leader or politician) – 'Ek (one) neta', 'Kayi (many) neta. Or they may be different, e.g., 'bachcha' (child), 'bachche' (children). Plurals also change with the case, e.g., 'Sapna' (dream), 'Sapne' (dreams), 'sapnon ka' (of dreams). In these translations, this complexity has generally been avoided by accepting the addition of 's', to make plurals, for instance, 'devatas' and 'raths'. The possessive noun has been used in both ways, with an apostrophe 's', 'panch's' and also in consonance with the first language, e.g., Pahari ('of /belonging to the 'Pahar' i.e., mountains). For this collection, the earlier versions of the translated stories: "Cats Talk", "The Reddening Tree", "Daarosh", "Saddle", "Savarna Devta, Dalit Devta", "Slur", and "In the Name of Gods", have been reworked by the editors with the consent of the translators. In doing so, the guiding principles have been those of lucidity and accuracy, especially of cultural concepts specific to Himachal.

Hence, we can say that the translated works have been able to retain the originality of the Hindi text but have also evolved it to suit the sensibilities of the readers that it caters to. e.g., 'saved me from clutches' is a Hindi expression 'change see bacchanal, 'pitcher' of water is culturally specific to India as the foreigners do not use a pot to store water, 'swallow his rage' is again the translated sentence in Hindi as 'Gussa nigal Jana'.

CHAPTER 3

Conventions and Contemporaneity

Conventions are a pattern of customs and traditions that are emulated in a particular manner and that have been accepted through the generations as a certain protocol in the social setup of any civilised community. They are rules or methods that have been adopted and established by usage, agreed and consented upon by a particular community in social situations or celebrations. A convention can also be described as the normal or accepted way of doing things a way of behaving that is generally accepted as being correct and right in context to societal and civic conduct. In the social context, a convention may be undertaken as an unwritten law of custom that is not formalised, though some conventions are legislated and documented, validating them to be followed strictly. A convention is a set of generally accepted standards, norms or criteria, that take the form of a custom. In social constructionism, there is a great focus on social rules. The standards of performing any social or religious activity become a traditional procedure that is neither disturbed nor challenged for the fear of their being shaken or changed. Any disparity may lead to confusion and further chaos in society which may be fraught with strife over this issue. Thus, to ensure the formal acceptance and adherence to these conventions, any sort of defiance is ignored, rejected, and in more serious situations even subjugated. This may lead to the conventions turning into a set of orthodox traditions that may look obsolete and abominable. The repression of any proposed change may look illogical and unreasonable to society. These rules are often socially constructed and applied to each member of society, but at the same time, are re-produced by individuals from time to time with the advent of discoveries, education, and progressive thoughts. Social rules are created through the interaction between the members of society. The focus on active interaction highlights the fluid, shifting character of social rules. These are specific to the social context, a context that varies through time and place. That means a social rule change over time within the same society. Rules and customs acceptable in the past may no longer be relevant to be followed. Similarly, rules differ across regions too; what is acceptable in one society may not be so in another.

Contemporaneity is the modern and the present way of living which is in contrast with the traditional methods that have long been followed. The present is different from the past and also prepares one for the future that is further apprehended to be different from the present. The key features of modernity are the rise of scientific and rational thought, individualism, industrialisation, and urbanisation. According to Dan Laughey, modernity may be categorised as the Early modernity from 1500 to 1789 when people were beginning to experience a more modern life, Classical modernity from 1789 to 1900 was marked by the rise and growing use of daily newspapers, telegraphs, telephones and other forms of mass media, which influenced the growth of communicating on a broader scale and Late modernity from 1901 to 1994 which consisted of the globalisation of modern life (Laughey 31). Late modernity is characterised by the highly developed global societies of today. Modernisation continues into the contemporary period and is marked by technological and social changes resulting in contemporary societies that are a continuation of institutional transitions and cultural developments. There is a post-traditional order in the modern world that instead of being in complete opposition to traditionalism, may be called classical modernism. This is the balance that is necessary for the conventions and contemporaneity to move along simultaneously in harmony. This may vary from region to region and influences the mountains and far-fetched rural areas later than the urban localities.

This research is an attempt to analyse the stories by SR Harnot, in the context of this transition and the impacts on the society dwelling in the mountains. The stories are originally written in Hindi and translated to English in the book *Cats Talk* edited by Dr. Khemraj Sharma and Dr. Meenakshi F. Paul. There are twelve stories in the book that have been translated. This work titled *Conventions and Contemporaneity: An In-Depth Analysis of the Translated Short Stories in S. R. Harnot's Cats Talk* aims at analysing the multiple issues that have cropped up due to the invasions of modernity in the quaintness of the hills and how the traditional inhabitants have responded differently to the new modes of life in cultural, social and environmental spheres as depicted very intricately in *Cats Talk*. It proposes to explore the conventions and traditions followed in the hills by the village folks and how these conventions confront the modern ways of livelihood. The collection of short stories by S.R Harnot is a translated work that has immersed itself in the social fabric and cultural flavours of the state of Himachal Pradesh and has touched every aspect of the people's sentiments adding a "local color" (Abrams201) to the text. "The detailed representation in the prose fiction of the setting, dialect, customs, dress, and ways of thinking and feeling which are distinctive of a particular region." (Abrams 201). The author, SR Harnot has told the tales that have adorned the mantle of the hilly lifestyles and its culture and can be called regional fiction. As defined by MH Abrams, "the term "regional fiction" is then used to distinguish those works which deal with more deep-seated, complex, and general human characteristics and problems" (201). The characters have been marginalised psychologically as a result of the changing pattern of society and due to the contemporary trends in the professional sphere. The stories may be set up in the region-specific to the hilly state but the concerns and the themes are universal, relevant, and applicable to the societies of all places. Due to the geographical locations, the uneven terrain, and harsh climatic conditions, people remain disconnected from the rest of the country for a few months of the year. These factors make the people quite vulnerable and sensitive to the evolving social conventions, not allowing them to get acclimatised, accustomed, adjusted, and adapted to the new scenario.

Conflicts between Conventions and Contemporaneity

Conventions are disturbed and sometimes challenged by contemporaneity which may be referred to as new changes occurring simultaneously at a particular period of time. This research work refers to the present modern ways that are contemporary to the lives of the people who have been portrayed in the stories. Contemporaneity seems to have impacted the environment adversely which has been studied in detail in the research. However, for the women and the subalterns, contemporaneity has improved their lives and brought a ray of hope to break away from the shackles of customs that have subjugated them through the ages. The deity's role however has been challenged in the stories but a balance is struck with events that remain mysterious.

It is an attempt to explore the conventions and traditions that the village folks follow in the hills and how these conventions conflict with the modern ways of livelihood that the younger generation would like to follow. Though still rooted in their traditions, there is no way they can continue with them in the urban areas where they shift, to attain higher education or to earn their livelihood. Looking at this from the casteist, feminist, environmental, and religious perspectives, it is observed that the conventions become difficult to be adopted in the same manner, and hence the relevance of these traditions has to be adapted to instill a few aspects of contemporaneity in them. The research proposes to explore this conflict and map its impact on the people's lives as depicted in the translated short stories of SR Harnot in the book *Cats Talk*. It would also describe the space where the conflict is compromised and balance is achieved. In the wake of the new generation striving to attain professional heights and explore their employability skills and capabilities, the old and ailing parents are left alone in their native villages and towns. Accepting the new norms of the societies, stories like "Cats Talk", "Ma Reads", "Twenty Feet Bapuji", and "m.com" deal with the complexities that arise in the lives of these parents who are forced to live a lonely life away from their children, eventually and gradually coming to terms with the realities of life, accepting their plight and proceeding with a determined will to be independent both financially and emotionally. The parents have accepted their loneliness and instead of complaining, have found solace by embracing the pet animals whom they look after and rear like their own offspring. The love and loyalty that they receive in return are priceless for them as the innocent animals don't understand the importance of attaining monetary benefits. The story, "Twenty Feet Bapuji" has epitomised the social degeneration that has taken place in the land of Bapu (Father) where the children have failed to recognise the value of their parents as their vision is blurred by the luster of the modern city life that they are leading in the cities not allowing them to get back to the supposedly mundane life of the rural areas. It strives to study the conventions which may be defined as the standards of our beliefs, and social norms and how these particular rules have been set up through the ages. They have been accepted as a pattern and method of performing activities and are considered and acknowledged to be correct. The conventions may or may not be rational or based on logical thinking but are never questioned or doubted for their authenticity or their credibility. They can either be customs of religious ceremonies or the rules set up for the society that marginalise women and subalterns. However, the conventions do have positive aspects attributed to them when it comes to the environment preventing any kind of pollution or damage. The old parents who are left behind in their homes also follow the traditional methods of livelihood that keep them rooted in their organic way of living, preventing any negative impact of modernity. Similarly, the worshiping of the local deities allows the people to remain religiously and ethnically inclined toward the conventions followed in the hills. So, it can be said that the impact of this has been a mixed one on society, allowing them to remain connected to the traditional and cultural ways and even letting them follow some social norms that have mutilated the self-respect of the marginalised classes, exploiting them economically and socially. Conventionally the hills have been described as aesthetically beautiful, being unexplored and unexploited, and in sync with the nature and environment.

The stories provide ample examples of the various conflicts that these traditions face with the trends of the new world that have disturbed the family structure and the dynamics of society. In the story "Cats Talk", Amma (Mother) is often worried about her son and his family who live in the city, and from the anecdotes of the postman, she gathers what life in the city is like. The author goes on to explain:

> How restless city life has become! Every day something nasty takes place there....How must her son and daughter-in-law be managing their lives under these conditions? And then, there's the little one going to school! This is why Amma loves her village where peace prevails all year round, no riots, no baton charge or police firing here. ...Even if her son has become a complete city man and the daughter-in-law hates to visit her, how she can forget them and their well-being! (Harnot 15)

Whereas, in the story "Twenty-Foot Bapu Ji", Harnot has explained another aspect to show how the new generation does not want to continue with the old occupation that the fathers had been into. They decide to settle down in the cities leaving their ancestral homes in the village. Chachu's son is an Army officer, which makes it difficult for him to accept his father as a Ghodewala. "But Chachu paid no heed. He did not leave his work; so, his son left him. He went away and never came back to the village or even to Shimla to look up to his father." (36)

In the story "m.com", the dilemma of the old Ma is depicted when she wants to dispose of the dead buffalo that was done by the village tanner earlier. This time when she went to inquire about him, the revelations made were quite surprising for her. She had to get her cattle registered if she wanted them to be disposed of by the government agencies. Modernity had penetrated so deep into the lives that even the cattle were dragged into the advanced system of being registered. The writer writes about what is going on in Ma's mind "Times have changed. There's hardly any courtesy or sense of right or wrong left in the village. Whatever little civility still exists is merely to keep up appearances. The boys of the new generation are rude to your face. They have no respect for elders. How many old people have left anyhow?" (Harnot 101). In another instance where the writer tries to depict the generational dissonance cropping up in society, the writer attempts to explain the same by depicting it in the story where the technological advancement has paved way for the new techniques that would reduce pollution caused by following the traditional methods earlier. "Tai! They will come in their vehicle. Pick up your buffalo from the shed and take it away…There will be no filth in the fields, no vultures, no rioting dogs. Ma's head was in a spin. The name of the shop was blazoned in bold letter-m.com machine" (Harnot 105)

The motif of newspaper and cow dung very well explains the comparison between education and rural lifestyle in the story. In the story 'Ma Reads', the old mother is living a traditional rural life but his son is rather surprised to know that his mother too reads what he writes. A writer in the city, her son doesn't share anything about his being a writer with his mother, but to his surprise when he visits her in the village, he finds out that all the copies of all his books are present in the house, kept nicely by his mother. The supposedly illiterate village woman, she is as updated about his writings as any other urban woman would have been. "Everything is becoming clearer; Ma is looking at the newspaper. The postman is pointing something to her in its centerfold. Ma carries the newspaper inside, puts it down somewhere in the cowshed, and starts to pile up dung as before." (Harnot 110)

The question of social absurdities can be viewed in the caste divisions of the society which hovers over like a challenge to the newly construed social milieu. Though the society claims to be progressing on the path of modernisation, these casteist hindrances often prove to be an obstacle, not allowing a comprehensive upliftment. The subalterns in the established hierarchy of the Indian caste system, are often deceived into believing that the new progressive world has rubbed away all the class distinctions. The archetype of casteist segregation co-exists in the minds simultaneously with the futuristic ethos of the people of the state who are determined and devoted to creating a modern society. The efforts of the government in this direction are exposed to be a farce and a mere nexus between the bigwigs of the system to reap the benefits of the whole business of development. The stories "The Saddle", "In the Name of Gods", and "Svarna (Gold) Devta (Deity), Dalit Devta" describe the underlying casteist divisions that continue to haunt society.

This conflict between conventions and the rebellion of the subjugated subalterns is another important theme that would expose the double standards and the hypocrisy of the upper caste when it comes to fulfilling their selfish motives as presented in the stories. The lower caste people are kept at bay by the upper caste men, but when they are needed for the accomplishment of the bigger projects, the upper caste men would not hesitate in upgrading their status and making them happy. One such incident has been depicted by Harnot in the story "The Saddle". In this story, the writer has portrayed the protagonist who protests against the Bhunda custom where a low caste man is elevated to the position of a Brahmin for a day when the life-risking ceremony of sliding from a mountain top to the deep gorge has to be performed on a rope that is made of grass. He is made a scapegoat and his family is compensated. But after the ceremony, he is again treated as an untouchable. In this story, the Sahju, as the man performing the ceremony is addressed, is intelligent enough to bargain for the lost land and properties at the right time when the ceremony was about to start in the presence of the CM along with a huge public gathering, and not agreeing to his terms could mean a big insult for the organisers. "Then return our lands, Sharma Ji. We want to settle here, in this very village from where your ancestors had chased us away.... But today the Beda can do or say anything...." (Harnot 97). A similar theme of the subaltern not being allowed to rise is seen in the story "Svarna Devta, Dalit Devta", where the protagonist belongs to the lower caste and is stuck between the choices of following the ancestral occupation of playing pipes or studying further to attain the modern education in school.

As described in the following lines from the story: "He (his father) wanted me to take over from him the duties of the temple musician and become even more famous. But I had no inclinations towards music and always pleaded with him not to force me to discontinue my school and allow me to pass at least high school." (Harnot 113)

The role of Devta (Deity) who is held in very high esteem by the people of the state is another theme that would be analysed in the stories aiming to traverse the religious aspects and mapping its relevance. All the important decisions regarding the village are taken after consultation with the Devta and his approval is sought before any function or ceremony. The stories have very delicately struck a balance between the modern necessities and the 'will' of the Devta which are shown in conflict with each other. The chapter would propose to study how the people have retained their faith in the Devta despite the government taking decisions that are not in favour of the environment around the village inhabited by the people who live on the edge and would bear the brunt of the developmental activities.

Searching for a Feminine identity, rising to be at par with the more powerful and authoritative set of patriarchal rules and conventions, and recognising the female existence has found itself a place in the stories like "Daarosh" and "Slur". These stories question the age-old customs, the male chauvinistic mindset of misjudging the bold and strong women, and the shaping up of the young female mind at the backdrop of all the social conventions that act as a social construct of defining the duties and laying down the expectations from her. The educated females, especially in the tribal areas, are shown to rise against the traditional customs that have been formed for the convenience of the society but have been mutilating the honour of the women for years. The women have been treated as mere objects who have no right to choose a partner. The young widows have also been looked at as women who are vulnerable to exploitation. The issue of a single mother has also been taken up. The story "Daarosh", refers to a custom of 'coerced marriage' and is called 'Daarosh Dublub' which means marriage by force. The protagonist Kaanam defies the tradition by hitting the boy who had come to abduct her. As the boy turns out to be the M.L.A.'s son, her father is annoyed with her to let go of such an opportunity. Kanam's father's reply displayed a patriarchal mindset. However, for the young people of this tribal area, this news won accolades for her. The writer says "The news spread far and wide that Kaanam had beaten the MLA's son half-dead. The older men and women of the area thought this act of Kaanam was against their culture and tradition but young boys and girls praised her in their hearts." (75). On the other hand, the story "Slur" deals with more than one theme of modernity and tradition. The feministic aspect and the concept of a single parent are represented very appropriately through a widow who had been exploited sexually by many people of the village and her son who was born a few years after her husband's death was not given a father's name. She fought the case in the panchayat and finally was able to expose all of them and secure admission for her son. Against the father's name, her name was written. This was certainly defiance of a very strong convention. In "Slur", the theme of single motherhood has been dealt with subtly and smartly, not to magnify the issue bringing it to a larger spectrum. "The headmaster opened the register. He turned a few pages and vehemently dipped the nib of the holder in the inkpot. Then he shook off the excess ink and stroked out the name of the child's father. He now wrote a new name.... Manu Dutt, son of Smt. Shyama Devi." (Harnot 144). In the story "The Reddening Tree", Munni, a young girl is not allowed to go to school for reasons that are so typical of an orthodox society. Even though her parents sent her to school, after class three, she was not allowed to carry on with her further studies as they thought that educating a girl is of no use. This was a way of crushing the small aspirations of a tiny girl Munni's whose academic future was curbed in "The Reddening Tree'.

> "No wonder Munni is adept at every household chore even at her tender age. She churns milk, makes maize and wheat rotis(bread), fetches water and forage, milks the cattle, works the millstone, and even takes grain to be ground at the watermill.... Munni, however, still longs to go to school. But Bapu doesn't let her. He believes there is no use in schooling a girl. He allowed her to attend school till class three. Then he withdrew her name. Ma used to remonstrate with Mathru for spoiling Munni by sending her to school at all. "There are children from all kinds of families in the school. Now our Munni will sit with low-castes. Even eat with them...." (Harnot 48)

The stories "Aabhi" and "The River has Vanished" indulge in the issue of environmental degradation and ecological imbalances as a result of the developmental activities carried out to allow the most interior parts of the hills to be connected with the mainstream of the state. The disappearance of a river due to the multipurpose projects and dams constructed for channelising the natural waters of the perennial rivers to the drylands has led to irreparable damage to the river's ecosystem that thrives on the bounties of nature. The bird 'Aabhi' has been bestowed with the divine duties of looking after the lake and keeping it immaculately clean. She has been performing and adhering to this committed obligation from time immemorial. The juxtaposition of environmental exploitation and conservation has been intricately woven symbolising the natural checks and balances. The inhabitants of the village that would be relocated after the construction of a dam take the charge of not allowing ecological imbalance to take place by protesting against the construction of the hydroelectric project. All of the above-mentioned instances are elaborated further in the chapters. They aim at depicting how there is a conflict between the conventions and contemporaneity in the society of today.

CHAPTER 4

Empty-Nest Syndrome in Left-Alone Parents: Interrogating Generational Dissonance and Materialism

This chapter evaluates the effect of empty nest syndrome on left-alone parents in general and the single parents who are living alone in the rural regions of the hilly states in particular. The syndrome is universal but its effect on the parents is as varied as their cultures and lifestyles; the responses being as diverse. How these parents cope and adapt to a new lonely life without expecting much from their children living in the cities is inspiring and motivating for others. Streaks of the Alienation Effect are found in the parents who feel very distanced from their children. An emotional impact can be felt among the readers who identify with the state of gloom and loneliness that these parents experience. The empty nest syndrome may be referred to as a feeling of gloom, loneliness, and grief that the set of parents feel when they are left behind in their homes by their young adult children for pursuing higher education or for employment in other places. Though most parents suffer from this syndrome when their children leave their homes, some more susceptible ones have already been the victims of unfavorable circumstances like unstable marriage, untimely death of a spouse, and witnessing a transition in life like retirement. It is observed that stay-at-home mothers are more prone to this syndrome though some studies reveal that the fathers too are unable to cope with the emotional transition that comes with the children moving out. According to Jana l. Raup and Myers Jane, this syndrome includes symptoms like anxiety, restlessness, insomnia, and stress. However, some parents experience graver symptoms of depression, a sense of loss of purpose, feeling of alienation and isolation, and other mental health issues regarding the child's welfare. Though this is an outcome of modernity creeping in, the ways that have been adopted by them are both conventional and modern.

The stories of S.R. Harnot have depicted the plight of the left-alone parents in the villages of Himachal Pradesh, particularly in four stories in *Cats Talk;* these stories are "Cats Talk", "Twenty Feet Bapuji", "Ma Reads" and "m.com.". All the protagonists in the stories are single parents whose spouses have passed away years ago and hence they have been left behind in their homes. Another peculiar feature about these characters is that they thrive in a rural backdrop. Though the protagonist, Chachu in the story, "Twenty Feet Bapuji" Chachu, lives in the capital city of Shimla, he hails from a village that he had left long ago.

To live normal lives, these single parents have adapted themselves to their lonely lives. While analysing the stories, the lives of these elderly characters have been evaluated to find how they lead their lives. There are several ways by which the empty nest syndrome can be coped with. Following their hobbies and interests, spending more time with family, friends, and professionals, helping them in restarting their lives sans their children are a few methods. It is also a good way to rekindle the relationship with the spouse without the stress and responsibilities of bringing up and raising a child. They can pursue reading or further studies and can even go back to work after retirement. Since the financial burden of a child is reduced, they can spend more money on their leisurely activities like traveling and socialising. These ways help in reducing the anxiety about their child and diverting their attention to more meaningful and purposeful pursuits. However, the parents depicted in S.R. Harnot's stories live in rural areas and have different ways of coping with their loneliness. There are four stories, "Twenty Feet Bapuji", "Ma Reads" ' and "Cats Talk" and "m.com" that deal with this particular theme of old age, empty nest, left-behind parents. These parents are all single and have managed to revive their lives with their fellow villagers, neighbours, and relatives; and also find companionship in the animals.

There are animals like cows, sheep, cats, horses, and birds that they rear and feed. Animals have replaced their children in their lives and they receive a share of love and affection from these parents. Another way to cope with loneliness depicted in one of the stories is the reading habit that a protagonist develops to enjoy reading the books written by her son. Besides these, the household chores and the relationship with the neighbours and fellow villagers are other factors that help the old parents to adapt to their lonely lives. In one of the stories, the protagonist Chachu is not only dependent on his horse for financial pursuits but also finds the said animal as a companion in the evenings when he is alone after work. The issue of parents being left behind in their empty homes is an effect of modernisation where children move out in search of better employment opportunities. However, the parents still would want to continue with their old and traditional ways of livelihood and would like to continue with their traditional occupations as well. Evangelia P. Galanaki explains how being lonely is painful: "In the domain of Psychoanalysis, solitude, as a state of being alone, has been described as a fundamental human experience and has been ascribed a plethora of meanings. From the psychoanalytic standpoint, loneliness is the painful experience of being alone" (71). In the wake of the new generation striving to attain professional heights and explore their employability skills and capabilities, the old and ailing parents are left alone in their native villages and towns. Accepting the new norms of the societies, the stories like "Cats Talk", "Ma Reads", "Twenty Feet Bapuji" and "m.com" deal with the complexities that arise in the lives of these parents who are forced to live a lonely life away from their children. However, they eventually come to terms with the realities of life, accept their plight and proceed with a determined will to be independent both financially and emotionally.

In all three stories, the parents are left alone and are single. This makes their living even more difficult and challenging. Being alone is a fear that they face in their unconscious minds, though they seem to be leading very normal lives, and it is only in some instances when they wish their children near to face a particular situation. They accept their loneliness and find solace by embracing the pet animals whom they look after and rear like their own offspring. The love and loyalty that they receive in return are priceless for them as the innocent animals don't understand the importance of gaining monetary benefits. The story, "Twenty Feet Bapuji" epitomises the social degeneration that has taken place in the land of Bapu where the children fail to recognise the value of their parents as their vision is blurred by the brightness of the modern city life that they are leading in the cities. As Celia Dodd, quotes the family therapist John Hills, "Letting go is one of the hardest things that parents ever have to do...because it is about separation, loss, and uncertainty about how the person you love is managing and whether they are safe.... parents don't switch off" (50).

In the story "Twenty Feet Bapuji", Chachu is a widower and leads an independent life, but strictly adheres to the Gandhian philosophy. The fact that many fathers still see themselves primarily as protectors and providers…"' she further adds "…. men's daily routines aren't affected to the same degree unless they've been the main carer. That's because most men are less involved with the domestic and organisational side of caring for kids-not just laundry and cooking" (93). It is traditionally believed that mothers share a special bond with the children and fathers remain elusive to the separation from the children. However, studies in the 1970s have found that the paternal side is more affected by this breaking up of the family structure. Lillian Rubin, an American psychologist writes in her book *Women of a Certain Age* "It may be fathers more often than mothers who are pained by the children's imminent or actual departure" (Dodd 96). Chachu misses his son miserably now, not being able to bear the humiliation that he faced before the Independence Day celebrations on the Ridge. It is now that he longs to meet his son and share his emotional trauma as he feels he has grown old and weak to face such social stigmas that have had a painful impact on him. The author writes about Chachu's bonding with the horse in the story:

> Chachu tries to tell himself that he has neither a son nor a daughter-in-law. Not even a grandson. He is alone. Only the horse is his. They mean the world to each other. They are family, everything. When he was younger, Chachu could bear all this. But he can bear it no longer. His son comes to his mind again and again. He longs to see him once, if only once. But he does not have his son's address and even if he had, Chachu wasn't sure if he would recognise the boy…. No-no, why wouldn't he know him? How can parents forget their children? His son's childhood flashes before Chachu's eyes…. Chachu throws himself at the horse's neck and weeps. The horse quietly takes in Chachu's emotional embrace. He feels love suffusing his being; only, he cannot speak. (Harnot 42)

Old age is often compared to childhood, and in this case, Bapu remembers his childhood and how he had lost his father at a very young age, driving him to the capital city of Shimla to earn a livelihood. As Evangelia P. Galanaki says that the fear of solitude is considered to be a universal human fear and Sigmund Freud (1917/1963) connects the anxiety with solitude and darkness in the following famous observation: "In children the first phobias about situations are those of darkness and solitude. The former of those often persists throughout life; both are involved when a child feels the absence of some loved person who looks after it" (407). This holds for Chachu who had this fear of loneliness and loss of a loved one since his childhood that persists all his life. As Harnot explains in the story:

> Chachu must have been thirteen when he first came to Shimla…Chachu's mother had told him that his father had passed away in a road accident. He was their only son…. Chachu came to Shimla from his village to seek work with a distant relative. The kinsman taught him how to look after his horse. One day he died of illness and Chachu was left alone. (Harnot 35)

The above lines show how Chachu had been a loner all his life, his childhood had been harsh, his wife too passed away, his daughters married and settled happily in their own respective homes and his son who was taught in an English school became an army officer, leaving him alone. Chachu, who earns his living by providing joyrides on the ridge to the tourists, wanted his son to build a house in the village but rather his son asked him to leave this lowly work of being a Ghodewala. Loneliness has been an integral part of Chachu's life. In the story "Cats Talk", Amma, a widow, lives alone in the house in her village. Though busy with the household chores, the darkness brings all the problems for her. As the writer says "Many a time Amma quarrels with the dark" (Harnot 9) She is unable to locate herself and her belongings. He further writes "The dark confuses her and she rubs the wrong end of the matchstick" (Harnot 9). Darkness is symbolic of the life that the old parents lead, not seeing a light of hope for their future. They have nothing to look forward to at their age when the children have settled and become independent, and have left their homes making them empty nests. As the writer says about Amma, "Amma would never go to the loft in the dark. She is afraid". The fear of the dark can also be recognised as the fear of the unknown. The writer calls this fear of Amma "misapprehensions" (Harnot 10). Amma also misses her husband whom she calls *Pita* (Father) the way her children used to address him. The night and darkness are the toughest phases of the day when she has to face the psychological effects of being left alone. "Sometimes, Amma suddenly wakes up in the night and is overtaken by an illusion" (Harnot 17). As he further says "Strange is Amma's lonely world" (Harnot 3).

CHAPTER 5

Conventional and Modern Methods of Coping with Loneliness by the Elderly Parents

Elders in the hills have found ways to lead a life that is dependent on the natural environment comprising of flora and fauna and have ensured the preservation of a lifestyle that stimulates their social skills and enhances community welfare. Their mental and physical pre-occupations cocoon them away from the stress of solitariness at an advanced age. The methods are discussed below.

Rearing of Pets

To combat this fear and loneliness, the characters in the stories of S.R. Harnot have made the animals their companions. It is the pet animals that these left-alone parents have adopted and found company in; as livestock in "m.com" or as a source of income in "The Twenty-Foot Bapu Ji" or as a pet with whom one could converse and shower love on in "*Cats Talk*." They love the animals, feed them and even talk to them as their family members. Roberta Erickson has elaborated on 'the significant other', a term he uses for the pets that the people keep, and emphasises how important they are for the elderly. According to him, keeping pets is a way of combating loneliness. He writes

> The most common reason people give for owning a pet is companionship, a desire for physical proximity, friendly interaction, and a sense of esteem for another living thing. Loss of companionship is widely acknowledged as one of the social problems of the aged. Elders, who are retired, widowed, separated from their families, or living in cities often have a special need for close companionship. Pet dogs, cats, and birds can serve this function. (Harnot 92)

He further elaborates, "Having a pet can satisfy the need to be needed. While pets give affection and act as social aids, they are also responsible. Animals genuinely depend on human companions and force them to consider such practical matters as food, shelter, grooming, health care, and safety" (Harnot 93)". "Pets also help in promoting the health and longevity of the elders" (Harnot 95). Erickson further discusses how the pets help the old parents to fight depression, enhance their sense of humour, and add to the "interest, variety and complexity" (Harnot 93) in their daily lives. In "The Twenty-Foot Bapu Ji", the horse is a means of livelihood for Chachu who now looks after and feeds him like his own child. As the writer in the story depicts, "Chachu went to his horse. He caressed his forehead tenderly. The horse became a child. His eyes dripped love. Only Chachu or the horse knew how this affection steeped into his whole body. Chachu gave the horse some water. He put a gram in his feeding bag and gave it to him. The horse began to munch the gram" (Harnot 34). The horse is a source of income for Chachu and he loves him dearly. He even refrains from riding on the horse that he owned as he thought it would "dishonour the back that provided his livelihood by climbing upon it" (Harnot 41). Chachu is not only emotionally connected to the horse but also understands how important it is as a source of income.

However, this relationship between the human and the animals can be seen in a different light in "Cats Talk" where Amma is surrounded by her pet animals like cats that even sleep with her on her bed, besides having the livestock in a shelter very near to her room. "That's how her day begins.... with her also wake up her cattle in the shed.... Birds take a cue from all this and start twittering and chirping in the courtyard.... Not to be left behind are the cats who start their racing bouts the moment Amma rises from her bed..." (Harnot 9). They are the cats who have the closest proximity to Amma as they even sleep on the same bed where Amma sleeps. She says "...you two keep snoring in the soft, warm bed!" (Harnot 10). The writer elaborates more on the relationship between the cats and Amma, upgrading this bond to that of a mother and her daughters, as she has even named them as she would do to her children. Amma bestows them with all her motherly affections and care. They are an integral part of her world which is bereft of any human relationship at home. "The cats are mother and daughter, one white and the other black. No one, not even Amma can ever tell which of the two is younger. One is called Kali and the other Nikki. The cats know their names because when called so, they respond immediately" (Harnot 10). The cows too start mooing as they hear Amma's voice in the morning. The cows in the cattle shed come to know when Amma wakes up and wait for her to attend to them and feed them fodder. The writer says:

> Even though the cowshed is at some distance from where Amma sleeps, the closeness between the two can be known from their conversations. Amma knows what the cow says or wants from her and reasons with her while lying in bed. Sometimes she even scolds her, 'Don't make so much noise, Chambi. Let me get up at least, I'll attend to you before doing anything else. (Harnot 11)

Amma's conversations throughout the day are made only with the animals that she is surrounded with. The feeling of loneliness doesn't creep in as they keep her busy all along. "Strange is Amma's lonely world. She is always busy with someone somewhere" (Harnot 13). She milks the cows, feeds the birds, cats, and cows, and does all the other chores for the cows and bullocks, and lambs. There are several animals that she has in her cattle shed. "In Amma's cattle shed there are other animals also-a pair of bullocks, one baby cow, and two lambs" (Harnot 11). Amma's conversation with the pets is no different than her talks with the birds that wait for her to feed them with grains. To keep the cats away from the birds that come to peck at the scattered food, Amma keeps a watch over them or fills their saucers with milk at the same time to keep them away from the birds. The writer further emphasises Amma's monologues with the speechless animals, "The whole village can hear Amma calling the birds any time of the day.... 'Come birdies, come, your food is waiting for you!'" (Harnot 12).

Amma does not only find solace in the company of the cats but also depends on the cattle to fulfill her daily requirements of milk. They have become a family for her; financially, socially, and emotionally. In the story "Ma Reads", the mother Ma, as she is referred to by her son, lives alone in her village home. The only way she passes her time is by doing the household chores and reading. In this story, we also observe that the animals in her cowshed are the only companions she has while she lives alone. The writer says "Her mornings are spent in the cowshed, feeding and watering the animals, milking the cows, heaping dung" (Harnot 106). In the story "m.com", the protagonist is a widowed old woman who has two sons, both working in far-off cities. Like Amma in 'Cats Talk" *and* Ma in "Ma Reads", the story "m.com" also depicts the loneliness of the mother, Ma. Like both the previous characters studied, this mother also lives alone in her village home, with only her pet animals as her sole companions. There is no other human existence in her house. She also wakes up every morning to the mooing of her cows and the chirping of birds in her courtyard. As her son visits her, he observes and writes about his Ma, "Morning times are very busy for Ma. The moment she wakes, birds begin to chirp again. The cat becomes excited about milk and buttermilk. The cattle moo in the shed and Ma talks with them from the kitchen" (Harnot 100).

Household Chores

There are other ways of coping with loneliness, one is facing this situation by doing the household chores all by oneself. This helps the women characters of the stories remain active physically and pre-occupied mentally. In the context of this method, Raup and Myers have elaborated:

> Black and Hill also discussed the significance of meaningful work involvement for women. They found the key determinants for women's adjustments to the post parental period to be the degree of involvement in the maternal role and the ability to cope with situations as they arose. The majority of women interviewed did not consider the empty-nest a traumatic experience. Rather, their attitude was one of anticipation, because additional time and energy would now be available for personal development. (Raup 181)

This helps us in understanding the sociological impact of an empty nest on the older women in the stories of S.R. Harnot. These characters have coped with the loneliness by keeping busy managing the hearth and cattle shed chores. Be it in the kitchen, the courtyard or the cattle shed, they have maintained a routine that is followed religiously owing to the responsibilities of the pets and the food that they cook on time. The rural setup is different from the comfortable and convenient urban life where people are more dependent on modern electrical gadgets to carry on their daily chores. However, the village women depicted in the stories have followed the traditional methods for years. The kitchens have conventional chulhas (Mud Oven) and these women use the wooden or cow dung fuel to keep the hearth burning. The food is cooked on the fire of the chulha and the water for washing is also heated up over it, making it the center of the household activity. However, arranging the fuel for the same is a task that requires time and hard work. Collecting wood and making cow dung cakes is a process that is peculiar to the villages alone. It's very subtly captured in the story "Cats Talk":

> Now Amma lights the fire. When the weather is fine during the summer, Amma makes the fire with a handful of dry grass but during winters or rains, she puts the dry *beul* (Plant)shoots or cow-dung play in the earthen fire-pot and covers them with ash to preserve it from going out. …. Amma remains preoccupied with the household activities throughout the day, not realising how the time passes. Except for the night, she never gets the time to feel lonely or lament about her situation or be fearful about anything. It's a child's play for her to tell the time of the day or night. It has become a habit for her to rise first in the morning. (Harnot 12)

Similarly, in the other story "Ma reads", the writer gives a glimpse into the world of his mother which may be bereft of any human existence but is charming in its way. Ma has her own cozy space which consists of her pets, cattle, her pattern of work, and her son's books. She even spins wool and plaits the dried date leaves to make various articles. "Ma lives here alone. The front door of the house has been left open today. On most days Ma is up early and out of the house, the door shut behind her, doing outside chores. Her mornings are spent in the cowshed, feeding and watering the animals, milking the cows, heaping dung" (106) "Ethos, World View, and the Analysis of Sacred Symbols" in the book titled *The Interpretation of Cultures* underscores the importance of the distinct worldview of people

> "A people's ethos is the tone, character, and quality of their life, its moral and aesthetic style, and mood; it is the underlying attitude toward themselves and their world that life reflects. Their world view is their picture of the way things in sheer actuality are, their concept of nature, of self, of society" (Geertz 127).

The above lines emphasise the importance of the ethnic ways and lifestyles that the people follow along with the symbolic representation of the culture. The symbols and ethnicity of the people contribute to the depiction of their culture. In the stories of S.R. Harnot, these symbols may be seen through the handicrafts and household utilities that are an innate part of the lives of the characters. The writer further elaborates how the mother in the story has her belongings scattered everywhere around her house, a testament to the artisanship and craftwork that she keeps herself busy with after the main house tasks are done.

> Things are scattered everywhere. Nothing is in its right place. On the right side of the door, as you walk in, there is a clay pot for churning milk…To the left is a basket stuffed with unspun sheep wool…A spindle is lying on the side. Date leaves are strewn in one corner and amongst them lie a few mats made from plaited date leaves. (Harnot 106)

The clay pots, the dried date leaves, plaited incompletely and the oil lamps are culturally specific symbols that also show a contrast between modernity and tradition. In the story "m.com", the protagonist Ma and her household work are depicted in the following lines:

> Morning times are very busy for Ma. The moment she wakes, birds begin to chirp the again. The cat becomes excited about milk and buttermilk. The cattle moo in the shed and Ma talks with them from the kitchen. Nowadays, Ma listens to the new bhajan album 'Kabir Amritvani' on the tape recorder... (Harnot 100)

Socialising

The characters in the stories of S.R. Harnot may not feel isolated and lonely during the days, owing to the society that they live in. The women characters are busy with the neighbours and the relatives who live around them in the village and often participate in all the social activities like wedding ceremonies or other functions. The neighbours even help these ladies if they ever fall ill, by feeding the cattle and helping with other chores. Chachu in "Twenty Feet Bapuji" is also surrounded by his fellow *ghodewallas* and the other people whom he meets every day on the vibrantly crowded Ridge. In today's world where people have virtual friends and socialise on social media, the Covid times have taught us how important it is to have real friends in flesh and blood around us. The advantage of living in rural areas is that people have a close-knit social setup where they often meet and share lighter moments almost every day. This human interaction is instrumental in the mental well-being of people. The psychological boost that people receive with such social communication contributes to helping them fight loneliness. In the story "Cats Talk", Amma industriously works throughout the day but is also socially involved with the people of the village whom she talks to when they pass by or the children who are fondly given something sweet by Amma. This is evident from the following lines from the story:

> Hardly is there any child in the village who has not eaten a piece of jaggery or butter-smeared roti from her hands. Hardly is there a woman who while going to fetch water or collect firewood has not stopped in Amma's courtyard for a puff of her bidi. There's not a dog in the village that has not tasted a few crumbs of roti with its quota of swearwords while passing by Amma's door or any bird that has not pecked the grains in her courtyard. Even stray animals would not forget to have a casual peep into her courtyard while passing by her house. (Harnot 13)

If it so happens that Amma doesn't feel well, the inhabitants of her small world help and cooperate in their own special and specific ways. The response of the villagers and the pets overwhelmingly presents a perfect picture of mutual understanding and harmony that the fellow villagers and Amma share. The following lines from the story illustrate how the society of the village is a welfare society:

> If Amma ever falls ill, then a woman or a girl from the village takes charge of her household chores, fetches water for her, and feeds her pets. Even cows and cats do not bother her when she is unwell. The birds take care not to make any noise and let her take full rest. …. As for the cats, they either quietly crouch around her or just lick her feet, legs, or hands. As for the bird party, it keeps flying around…chirp, and sing around her as usual for they also wish to be near her when she is sick or unwell….it is the collective good wishes of her pets that Amma soon gets well. (Harnot 13)

Amma is not the only character who is helped by the villagers. The other character is that of Ma in "m.com" whose buffalo dies suddenly. The disposal of the dead animal becomes challenging for her when she realises that the new system would require her to get her cattle registered so that they become eligible for proper disposal by the government. However, before she learns all this, she talks to the old leatherworker who used to help the people in doing so. However, with the changing times, they have stopped doing it. Nevertheless, Ma is helped by the people she speaks to regarding the disposal. "The news of the buffalo's death had not reached the village or the women would have come by now to mourn its passing. Ma had not told anyone. Had she so wanted, she could have asked a village boy to go and hail the leatherworker but at this time she thought it best to go herself." (Harnot 100)

The villagers are very social and helpful and would have rendered any kind of services for Ma that would be required by her in any situation. When she reaches the leatherworker's house, she is told that he no longer indulges in the disposal of animals. Even his sons have not continued with this traditional practice of their family. But she is guided by the leatherworker who asks her to meet his son who owned a shop in the bus station. Ma reaches the bus station and manages to locate his son Mahendra's shop with the help of Budhram. Mahendra then searches for her name on the computer and informs her that neither she nor her animals' names were on the list. Further Budhram also explains to her the whole process by which the registered animals are included in the list, and how in case of their death an email is sent to the authorities who would send a vehicle and remove the dead animal from the cowshed. He also tells her that unlike the old methods of taking away the skin and leaving the rest for the vultures in the fields, these people would carry away all the parts of the animals so that there is no pollution.

Reading

Other than these conventional and traditional lifestyles, another aspect of the old parents that the story throws light on is the reading. The books that Ma reads in the story "Ma Reads", when she is done with or doing her household and outside chores show her love for reading. However, the writer of all her books is her son who has now become a famous writer in his own right. She has been able to get the newspaper and the books delivered to her doorstep by the postman of the village Amru, who keeps her updated about the writer's latest books. He also brings the daily newspapers for Ma every day.

Reading is one way to fight loneliness and the characters in the stories of S.R. Harnot have dwelled in their rural environment. Loneliness is something that they have experienced after their spouse's death and their children's leaving homes but they have managed to adapt themselves well to this in their unique ways. Ma in the story "Ma Reads" finds time to read any time of the day and not just in one room or at night. Such is her excitement to read her son's books that she can find time even in between her daily routine work to read his books. The writer finds out that his mother has been reading his books that he has never told her about. This secret is well-kept by Ma as well who also doesn't discuss the books with him. The writer discovers about his mother reading his books which is expressed beautifully by Harnot in the following lines:

> I take the first book in my hands. I turn the pages. Pressed between them are blades of grass, and butterfly wings. When Ma goes out to cut grass, she must sit there leafing through its pages. I pick up the second book. It carries the sweet smell of mustard flowers … I flip through and find yellow flowers stuck in places. There's also an occasional sprig of wheat. When Ma goes to the fields to pick greens, she must sit there and turn its pages. Now I pick up the third book. It's a novel I wrote. The fragrance of Raat ki Rani starts to fill the room. My eyes drift across the courtyard and I spot the plant. How tall it's grown! Its branches have spread everywhere. My mind wanders to the past. Summer nights, awash with the light of the moon, often saw Ma haul me onto her lap and tell me stories … Flowers from the Raat ki Rani are preserved between the pages. Ma must sit under its shade and read this book on moonlit nights.

> The fourth book is immersed in the smell of buttermilk and flour. The pages carry the impressions of fingers still sticky from the dough. In places, the words have become illegible from butter grease. Ma must look upon it while cooking Rotis or churning milk. The fifth book is now in my hands. Its pages have the whiff of the dark about them, the smell of bidi seeped inside. I observe the pages and turn them over. The words have dissolved and disappeared in places. In between is the residue of ash from a lit bidi. A dead firefly is stuck in one place.... perhaps Ma holds it in her hands on a moonless night and reads...beads of sweat form on my forehead. This book has several pictures of my father too...Ma must share her writer son's success with his father in her memories. I put this to one side and start searching for the pillow again. In the folds of the bed, I find yet another book. I take it out. This is my seventh book. My surprise knows no bounds. This is the new book that was launched only a week ago. Its pages smell of cow dung. Impressions of dung-stained hands are left here and there. Strands of white sheep wool are stuck in a few places. Ma must sit in the cowshed, amongst the animals, and look at it. (Harnot 109)

According to various kinds of research done in Australia, interviews were conducted on people aged sixty-five and above to know what their pastimes were and how they cope with loneliness, it was found that reading was one way in which they tried to do so. The researchers found reading to be one of the 'solitary' activities often mentioned as a useful pastime. 'If the interviewees could be viewed as self-medicating to alleviate feelings of loneliness", the study notes, "the most common medicine reported was booked." 25 Participants discussed how "reading allows them to remain cognitively active while engaging in an enjoyable and appropriate use of time. (Hilhorst et al 12). Similarly, surveys conducted in other countries also suggest that the older generation has learned how to combat loneliness through the habit of reading books. Though socially connected with society and their neighbours, the character of Ma has found ample time to read the books that her son has authored. According to Demos and The Reading Agency, "reading has been demonstrated to significantly reduce feelings of loneliness across age groups" (Dixon et al). "A Dutch study found a similar link between different leisure activities and the reduction in social isolation and loneliness... The Australian and the Dutch studies both suggest that reading combats loneliness by offering a worthwhile pastime" (Hilhorst et al 12) Though the people surveyed in Australia have a completely different setup where they are connected to the world online and may even have an opportunity to read the books on the internet, the rural society and people where Ma resides are not as aloof as the urban population where one can feel alienated. The books are delivered to her by the postman, which is a conventional way of communicating in today's modern world.

However, Ma helps in establishing the fact that the habit of reading is universal. The reasons for Ma to read her son's books are very personal to her but that has certainly helped her to overcome the situation where she is living alone in her village home without her son around. This may be one of her ways to remain in touch with her son and feel his presence in the house. Being far away from her son, the books give her an ample opportunity to read and understand the thoughts that are expressed in his writings. Reading interventions can be a powerful tool in the battle against loneliness. Of course, reading can be, and very often is, a solitary pursuit; of just one person curled up with a book. But when people come together to talk about books it is a social activity too. In both cases, reading helps people cope with isolation and reduce loneliness. Moreover, the evidence suggests this can be beneficial for many different groups – young and old. It stands to reason then, that reading should be considered one of the foremost ways in which we should look to address the growing challenge posed by loneliness. (Hilhorst et al 15)

Though Ma has not been able to discuss the books with her son because of the books that he gets published, she has been receiving them through Amru the postman. She receives the newspapers also every day from the postman which makes her daily interactions with him necessary. The postman is like the source of all information for Ma. He is the link that keeps her connected to the outside world through the newspapers and also enables her to know about her son's recently published books. "Ma Reads" is another story that shows how the protagonist is kept well-informed by the postman regarding her son's books in the newspaper. Her son buys a parcel of all his books this time, but he is surprised to know that though he had never told his mother about his published books, he discovers all of them under her pillow and in her room. But Ma also doesn't embarrass her son by letting him know that she has read all of his books. This is all due to the postman Amru, because of whom she is well apprised of the writer's accolades and ordering the books and delivering the book parcels to her. Besides connecting to the outer world, another benefit of reading is to remain intellectually active by remembering or reasoning. According to research done on people, it has been found that reading is beneficial for well-being and a very healthy and stress-free life.

'Reading supports health outcomes in at least three distinct ways. Firstly, reading correlates with a better ability to understand health information. This in turn leads to better health outcomes across different conditions. Secondly, reading can directly affect wellbeing, as it seems to help to regulate one's mood and exercise the brain, possibly holding off mental health disorders and even dementia. Finally, reading for empowerment – for example, using self-help books – is known to be an effective way of supporting those with depression, anxiety, and anger issues. (Hilhorst et al 16)

Conclusion

Therefore, we can say that the dilemma of the older parents as they oscillate between conventions and contemporaneity has been portrayed as elaborated in the stories. It has tried to depict the ways in which they cope with the changing times. Generational dissonance is evident from the fact that the children have migrated to cities in search of better employment opportunities and educational avenues for the future generation. This leads to disharmony in the relationship between the old-age parents and their children and creates distance. Parents are forced to adopt modern and unfamiliar ways. However, the conventional methods that they adopt to keep their loneliness away help them to strike a balance between modernity and traditions. The villagers, animals, and the traditional methods of carrying out the household chores help them to fight loneliness and not depend on their children for emotional and financial needs. Another aspect that has been explored in this chapter is a reading habit that a character had developed in order to read her son's stories in the books that had been published. It depicts the connection between the older and the new generation. This was a surprise for the son who had not known that his mother too could read. He had assumed that his mother would never know about his literary endeavours and achievements, but to his utter surprise, he found all his books that were published in her room. The writer has portrayed the balance between the contemporary social changes and the traditional methods of livelihood. The impact on the characters has been captured well by the author. The balance has been brought by the traditional and the modern ways of living.

CHAPTER 6

Casteism in the Mountains: Depiction of Conventional Dominance over the Subalterns

This chapter looks into the treatment meted out to the subalterns by the higher classes has been depicted vividly taking the excerpts from the text of the stories. The efforts made by the young characters in the stories who have received education from schools and colleges have led to the change in the conventions that were being followed through the ages.

Subaltern Studies

Before analysing the stories in the context of education, the concept of subaltern studies will be focused upon. The term "subaltern" was conceived by the Italian Marxist Antonio Gramsci, who used it as a codeword for any class of people, especially peasants and workers, subject to the hegemony of another more powerful class. The term has evolved since its first usage by Ranajit Guha who used it to refer solely to peasants who had not been included in the mainstream capitalist system. It now refers to any person or group of inferior rank based on race, class, gender, ethnicity, or religion. The term has been adopted by a group of Postcolonial Studies scholars who formed a smaller group within the field known as Subaltern Studies following Gramsci's idea, to examine the formation of subaltern classes in the context of India and its near neighbours, providing a kind of counter-history, to address the imbalances and discrepancies of 'official' histories, which tend to focus exclusively on the affairs of the state and the ruling class.

This narrative strategy most clearly inspired by the writings of Gramsci was explicated in the writings of their mentor Ranajit Guha, in his manifesto in Subaltern Studies, and also in his classic monograph The Elementary Aspects of Peasant Insurgency.

Although they are, in a sense, on the left, they are very critical of the traditional Marxist narrative of Indian history, in which semi-feudal India was colonised by the British, became politicized, and earned its independence. In particular, they are critical of the focus of this narrative on the political consciousness of elites, who in turn inspire the masses to resist and rebel against the British. Instead, they focus on non-elites – subalterns – as agents of political and social change. They have had a particular interest in the discourses and rhetoric of emerging political and social movements, as against only highly visible actions like demonstrations and uprisings. The subalterns in India had been subjected to innumerable atrocities of various kinds in the social and public spheres through the ages and have also been responsible for letting the hegemonic and feudalistic society exist. As Vidyasagar Sharma elaborates:

> Subaltern classes include peasants, tribes, women and other groups denied access to get hegemonic power. Historically speaking, Subaltern studies defined themselves as an attempt to allow people to speak. Under Subaltern studies, a new kind of writing has been started. The Subalterns have allowed speaking and sharing their pains, anger, sufferings, and experiences which was denied by the elitist historians and scholars. The Subaltern scholars try to make an alternative history writing in which history would be written from below rather than from above. In the domain of literature, we can trace the root of subalternity. In the narration of Premchand writing subaltern subject such as peasants, women and Dalits makes their strong presence. But Subaltern as an autonomous domain of history and cultural studies emerged against elitist historiography of the Western world. In post-colonial India, the Subaltern studies are reflected in the various forms of writings of history and literature. So, subalternity becomes a dominant framework in literature when the marginalised section of the society has no voice of its own. (Sharma 3786)

The branch of literature and literary studies that deal with subaltern literature is also known as Dalit literature in India. The term 'Dalit' is believed to be used by Jyotirao Phule. The word means divided, split, broken, scattered, and literally, it could mean the oppressed class. This word was popularised by Dr. B.R. Ambedkar who used it to refer to the downtrodden people and this term was later revived by the activist organisation in 1972. However, Gandhi used the term 'Harijan 'to refer to these exploited and marginalised people. The term Harijan was coined by Narsingh Mehta, a Gujarati poet-saint of the Bhakti tradition, to refer to all devotees of Krishna irrespective of caste, class, or sex and some believe it was originally coined to refer to the children of the exploited Devadasis. SR Harnot is a writer from Himachal Pradesh who is a pioneer of Dalit literature. In his stories, he has delved deep into depicting the plight and the social stigma that the various castes who are marginalised face at every step. However, his stories have emphasised the bold resistance that the younger generation has put up by not conforming to biased conventions. The problem arises here when the retaliation from the subalterns is countered strongly leading to a fiasco. However, the writer has penned down the characters who are capable of handling the same and maneuvering the situation in their favour.

This chapter focuses on the other castes of Himachal Pradesh like the weavers, the clarinet players, and the untouchables who were made a Brahmin and a scapegoat for a day to perform a religious ceremony. The discrimination and defiance have very well been depicted in the earlier writings by Omprakash Valmiki in the book *Joothan* and by Sharankumar Limbale's *The Outcaste*. However, the stories of SR Harnot have also dealt with the other issues of Dalits like the gods of the lower classes who have been outcasted as well. The weaver's son and the clarinet player's son who are not encouraged to pursue further studies owing to their financial conditions is another issue that is dealt with in the stories. SR Harnot has tried to depict the plight of the marginalised people in the stories very sensitively and yet he has also managed to portray that the hostility is met with intense retaliation from the lower caste people.

The stories portray how the subalterns in the villages of the hills have been ill-treated and marginalised in society by the privileged high-caste people. The subalterns in the stories are depicted as people who are weavers, clarinet players, and farmers. The stories that would be taken up under this theme are "The Saddle", "Savarna Devta, Dalit Devta", and "In the Name of Gods".

There is a stark similarity between Om Prakash Valmiki's Joothan and the stories of Harnot who has captured the very essence of the Dalit exploitation and retaliation. In the story 'Svarna Devta Dalit Devta', the protagonist belongs to the family of the traditional clarinet players or the shehnai as it is called. The instrument is played during all the religious ceremonies and yet the pipe players are marginalised. Playing the shehnai is an integral and important part of any religious ceremony without which it may be considered incomplete. However, the clarinet players who are contributing largely to these ceremonies are treated as subalterns. Though extremely talented in the musical art form, instead of being rewarded or eulogised, these musicians have not been recognised for their work. The writer explains: "Father was known for his musical talents, especially his soulful shehnai recitals. In the entire Dalit community in and around the village, there was no one to match his shehnai skills." (113)

The tradition of exploitation has long followed and the recent incident, that had remained fresh in the memories of people, has been narrated in the story. The rules set by the higher castes were strictly adhered to and disobedience of any kind was dealt with very seriously to set an example for others. One character Shibbu Mistri, who was another skilled worker, had touched the chariot during a religious ceremony which resulted in his banishment ultimately. When he was asked to sacrifice a goat in punishment, for his inability to do so, his lands and property were confiscated by the higher caste people. The higher castes are exposed here as the writer contemplates the use of Shibbu's lands and his ornaments that were now adorned on the deity's statue and were not considered impure as it was touched and the lands tilled by the untouchable. The financial benefits derived from the exploitation of the Dalits were the real motive behind the punishments and the banishments. The following lines from the text would help in understanding the suffocating environs in which the Dalits are not allowed to thrive expressed effectively by the author.

> Shibbu Mistri stood in a corner and waited for his turn. In the meantime, the crowd pressed from behind. Shibbu lost his balance and lurched forward but somehow managed to hold back; but in the process, his hand touched the wheel of the chariot and it was noticed by the Thakur. Shibbu was dragged from the crowd and mercilessly beaten as if he had touched the chariot deliberately. Blood was dripping from his mouth and nostrils but nobody came to his rescue. The crowd was furious and clamoured to punish Shibbu severely. The incident was deeply etched in my mind. As atonement for his sin, Shibbu was ordered to sacrifice and offer a goat to the deity. When he expressed his inability to do so with folded hands, the panchayat told him that in that case, he would have to offer himself for sacrifice…The panchayat ordered him to leave the village and Shibbu had no choice but to pack up his little belongings and say goodbye to his ancestral village. (Harnot 127)

The ill-treatment of the subalterns or the low caste people has been depicted in the story where they are not allowed to enter the temples, even though they have been contributing by playing pipes for the temple ceremonies. The protagonist is the son of a clarinet player who was known for his musical talents. However, they are restricted from entering the temple, and in case anybody tries to break the rule, intentionally or unintentionally, the punishment rendered is harsh physically as well as mentally. One such incident narrated in the story gives a clear picture of the kind of treatment that the low caste people are subjected to if they ever try to break any convention or do anything that would challenge the established social norms defying which would shake the very foundations of the caste system.

> I sat down on the steps of the temple. When the priest noticed me, he was furious. He came running towards me and gave me a hard slap on my cheek. Then he caught hold of me, dragged me to my father, and almost threw me on the ground before him. And father, instead of protesting at the priest's behaviour, gave me one more slap. I cried for some time, …In no time rumour got around that the low-caste shehnai player's son was a rascal and had behaved disrespectfully with the priest. This incident dismayed me so much that I began to hate the brahmin students of my school and when safe I would play all kinds of pranks on them to tease and humiliate them. The brahmin boys took revenge by abusing and taunting and calling me by my caste. (Harnot 115)

The above incident is an example of the caste hierarchy that exists through generations based purely on the profession of individuals. The protagonist is humiliated and punished harshly and his deed is reported to his father who is expected to educate his son regarding the rules of society and religious places. This is a vicious circle of casteism which doesn't allow anyone to liberate himself from the shackles of this system. The parents don't support their children to pick up arms or defy any of the set traditions. Another incident is narrated in the story which throws light on the prevalence of untouchability that exists in society. People belonging to the low caste are considered to be impure and contaminated due to the lowly jobs that they were engaged in. However, with changing times and the coming up of modern technology, the nature and means of carrying out these works have changed. Considering the altered circumstances, untouchability has lost its relevance. Therefore, continuing with the age-old customs need not be followed blindly. Instances from the text depict how the protagonist was reprimanded for not letting the priest's wife cross the narrow path when he also was crossing the same. Due to the narrowness of the lane, they both happened to touch each other. This was made out to be a big issue by the priest's wife who considered it an insult for her to be brushed by the clarinet player's son. She accused him of doing this on purpose to make her impure and had expected him to stop and wait for her to cross the narrow path first. The pitcher of water that she carried was thrown away by her and she made a hue and cry of this incident, calling the attention of all the villagers so that the protagonist could be punished. This is evident from the following lines:

> One day the second wife of the priest...was coming back from the village well with a water-filled pitcher and in the narrow lane, I collided with her without any design. The lane was so narrow that two persons coming from opposite directions could not cross without colliding unless one of the two turned back to allow the other to pass. She had seen me coming from the other end of the lane and warned me to let her pass but I was adamant and asked her to turn and walk back. She paid no attention to my words and continued advancing. Since I was in no mood to oblige her, I also did not turn back and instead managed to cross the lane almost rubbing shoulders with her. No sooner had I crossed the lane than all hell broke out. She threw down the pitcher on the ground and began shouting and abusing them. (Harnot 115)

The above lines also subtly hint at the hypocrisy of the higher caste by referring to the priest's wife as the second one specifically. Another aspect of casteism is the continuation of the traditional practices of adopting the professions of the parents. The children are not allowed to pursue their studies as the parents think that education would stray them away from their traditional practices of playing the clarinets. The income derived from the profession is the economic aspect and reason for following the practices, but the social aspect is emphasised when the high caste people think that the discontinuation of their traditions would allow the children of the low caste to enter the dominion of the others and hence threaten their position. "They seemed delighted at the idea of my giving up school to play with the temple musicians." (116). This shows how elated and glad the high caste people felt when the protagonist wasn't allowed to pursue further studies. Entering the temple is another issue and treating them outside the temple compound is another. Restricting them to enter the temple is followed strictly by the priests, but another perspective that is depicted in the story is the inhuman conditions that the people are subjected to when they are invited to the religious ceremony to play the musical instruments but are made to remain out in the open like animals, without any roof or any cover from the harsh and cold climate. Whereas proper arrangements were made for the upper caste people, the musicians were left in the open to the mercy of nature. This is an example of their insensitivity towards their fellow beings. The following lines from the story would throw more light on the same:

> There was no proper arrangement for the musicians to sit and perform although there was plenty of space in the field. There was a small tarp spread on bamboo sticks on one side of the field and the rest of it was open to the sky. The entire attention of the organisers was on making the best possible arrangements for the deity's chariot and priests and the upper caste devotees…. The weather was cold but no arrangements for the fire were made and people were made to sit in the open in the cold. …we, the poor musicians, had no warm clothes and could fend off the cold only by sitting near the fire. To sit in the open in the freezing night with dew and frost falling from above, the very thought of it made one shiver. (117)

Not letting a Dalit enter the courtyard has been mentioned by Harnot as something which is usually not practiced. Premchand in his story *Deliverance* has portrayed the protagonist Dukhi who is made to work in the courtyard but when he dies and his body is not touched by any Brahmin nor is any Dalit willing to lift it for the fear of police. To show this aspect in his story, Harnot tries to tell how stringently the Brahmins of that village practiced untouchability so much so that humanity was put at stake.

> We had also heard that the Brahmins of this village hated the Dalits much more than anywhere else and did not allow them to enter even their courtyards. While we waited helplessly and watched the activities of the organisers, the upper caste people who had come to watch the pooja were amply provided with blankets, quilts, and even braziers to keep them warm. Meanwhile, the cold was increasing and at least I was getting worked up at the apathy and indifference of the organisers. We looked around but nothing was to come our way. My fellow musicians covered themselves with their torn and tattered cotton shawls and fell asleep. (Harnot 117)

This kind of disparity was shown not only to the people belonging to low caste but also to the Devtas of these people. Devta is the local god specific to a particular village, region, or community. The identity of the Devta is related to the people of that specific area or community, and hence they are their representatives. "Every devta or devi lays down rules that determine the daily lives of villagers, and which the people of that locality abide by. This forms the basic structure of the region's social organisation. The devta assigns work to different people according to their caste." (Sharma et al)The higher the caste, the better treatment the Devta is meted out with. The distinction made based on caste is carried out not only for the people but for the gods as well. The devtas of the Dalit classes are made as dwarpals or gatekeepers who are in a subordinate position and have minimal clothing on them and do not have a roof above their heads.

This is also justified by making people believe that these devtas hate clothes on them and feel restricted in the closet of the temple. The other one has no statute and the reason assigned is that they hate to have one for themselves. The third devta is identified by a mere conical stone slab that is fixed to the ground. It is adorned by an iron chain. The chief deity has three attendant deities, who are his gatekeepers. The first dwarpal, represented by a beautifully carved black stone statue, stands near the main door of the sanctum. He is naked except for his phallus which is covered with a piece of cloth. He stands in the open without any canopy. It is believed that he doesn't like clothes and hates being enclosed in a temple and that is why he stands under the open sky. The second dwarpal has no statue because he doesn't like one. He is identified by a conical stone slab fixed in the earth with a platform built around it. An iron chain is wound around the stone slab. The third dwarpal is identified only by an iron bar, thick and long and stuck deep into the earth. (121)

The following lines taken from the story sheds enough light on the disparity made in the form of offerings of food and lamps, ornaments, clothes adorned by the idols, and even the position given to them in the temple where they are made subordinates of the gods of the high caste. Harnot has depicted the same in the following lines where he explains the system of donating according to the recognition of the deities.

> These dwarpal receive no gold or silver offerings and no earthen lamps are lighted with ghee for them. The devotees, Brahmins and non-brahmins alike, who throng the temple to seek the fulfillment of their wishes, offer them coarse flour or iron bracelets. Earthen lamps of the coarsest oils are lit for them. They are also not offered tastefully cooked food but only thick Rotis made of the coarsest grains. No coconuts, dates, saffron, or betel nuts are given to them. All those costly things such as gold or silver or ghee lamps or ghee-cooked food routinely offered to the chief deity and his companions inside the sanctum are practically forbidden for these dwarpals and thus a strict hierarchy is maintained even in the house of gods. (121)

The priests of these Dalit gods and the worshippers who are Dalits themselves are not allowed to touch their foreheads to offer obeisance to these gods and are only limited to the thresholds of the temple and the dwarpals. There is a distinction made among the priests as well which clearly shows how marginalisation is practiced at every level. The author says

> Not only in this, but hierarchy is also strictly adhered to in matters of selecting the goors. For the chief deity, only a brahmin goor can be

appointed because he enjoys the highest status and has a place of privilege in matters of rituals and offerings. For other deities who are housed outside the main sanctum, there are non-brahmins, even Dalit priests, who have the same low status in the temple affairs as the deities they are appointed to serve. The village elders say that the chief deity is the only wish-fulfilling deity and also the tutelary devata of the entire village community. But we Dalits have never had the good fortune of touching even the threshold of the temple. We also wish to light a lamp before our deity, we also want to make offerings to him, but we are not permitted to enter the temple or touch the temple threshold with our foreheads. We bow to him only from the outside and seek his blessings from afar. The nearest that we can go is where the dwarpals stand, offer all our gifts to them, and come back home. (Harnot 121)

The devtas are discriminated against by observing strict hierarchy in the place of worship, where on the one hand the idols of the Dalit gods are installed outside the temples, to face nature's extremities and be laden with dust whereas on the other hand the idols of devtas of the upper Svarna caste are seated in the heart of the temple, high on the pedestal of the sanctum. The Dalit gods are adorned with iron bands whereas the Svarna devtas are decorated with rich ornaments made of gold and silver. The offerings made by the followers are scrutinised and it is assured that valuable offerings are made to the Svarna devtas whereas the Dalit devtas have to suffice with less. All this is done under the strict eye of the priests who keep a close watch on the happenings and people are afraid to anger them as this would mean inviting the fury and curse by the priests that they fear would ruin their lives. The following excerpts would throw more light on the same.

Thus, there are Dalits even among devtas, caste hierarchy even in the house of God. The savarnas have appropriated the gods and they swiftly climb the temple stairs without any let or hindrance as if the deities belong to their clan. And what doubt can there be? The way they swagger in claiming their right to the devta, they probably have it. The Dalits are just like the dwarpals, standing outside at the gate in the open, in cold or scorching sun, without any canopies or ornaments. Frost falls on them; storms cover them with dirt and dust. As for ornaments, they have only crudely made iron bracelets or waistbands. Offer them one such bracelet or waistband and the poor things are mightily pleasing. But you cannot please the chief deity with such cheap offerings. He is seated in the heart of his imposing temple surrounded by every possible luxury. And who would ever dare to offer him such things and incur unremitting humiliation and disgrace by his curse! (Harnot 122)

Moving to the next story, 'In the Name of Gods', the protagonist and his family are traditional weavers who have been living off their professional earnings which are very meager. Yet they never think of educating the next generation as this means that their source of income would be disrupted by the time that would be wasted in education. This fixation on one profession through the ages was a reason why they can never get out of the vicious circle of poverty. They continue to be the proletariat class that is at the mercy of the rich and the dominant class who pay them the money for their skilled work. The following lines depict how the parents would not want their sons to get educated and earn a better livelihood.

> Father was not in favour of allowing Som to continue his studies beyond class eight. He wanted him to marry and settle down in life. He also wanted that Som should now relieve him and take over the household responsibilities and look after the crops and cattle. He was a famous weaver of that area, who had his handloom and was known all over the place for his unmatched skill in weaving woolen wrappers, mufflers, and coat-patti lengths. (Harnot 146)

Just like the protagonist of the previous story, the main character Som, is a son of the traditional professional weaver and is expected to continue with the same occupation that would help the family to be financially independent. Any change in the profession is not encouraged either by the parents or the society as the ripples caused by such changes would create disturbance in the lives of the people of the village. Already the terrain of the hills is such that there is a risk at every step and in every form that one can imagine which made it even more difficult for Som to go to middle school which added to the woes of the protagonist. As he explains the woes in the following lines of the story:

> Som managed to pass high school in extremely trying circumstances. He could never have enough money for books and stationery and then there was the time wasted commuting between home and school on foot....high school was about eight kilometers away so the boys and girls of the village would not continue their studies any further. Moreover, the road to the junior school was stony and bumpy and passed through a patch of thick forest. Apart from the fear of slipping into a gorge, there was also the fear of wild animals. Then there flowed a hilly river close to the school which remained practically dry in the summer months but became a terror during monsoons and the students had to cross it to reach the school. (Harnot 146)

The dynamics of the caste system existing in the village are elaborately described in the story. It is worth mentioning here that the Svarna class is in minority in the village and yet they have managed to rule over and dominate the Dalits. The Dalits who are illiterate and poor are exploited by the upper caste who drag them into the vicious circle of loans on the money borrowed. Though in the majority, the Dalits are further bifurcated into sub-castes which makes things more complex for them in the village. The land is owned by the Swarna caste people who utilise it to their benefit by exploiting the poor. We can relate this to the Marxist theory where the social superstructure doesn't allow the economically backward class to rise against the capitalist model where the rich gets richer and the poor is rendered poorer.

> The village was small and the dominant people, though numerically a minority, were either brahmins or thakurs whose writ ran unchallenged in the village panchayat. They had money, they owned most of the agricultural land and they were also in the money lending business but they were self-centered and could not think beyond their petty selfish interests. They took full advantage of the poor Dalits' misery and illiteracy. The Dalits, though a majority, were divided into numerous sub-castes. They were always at the mercy of the savarnas who exploited them in every conceivable manner. (Harnot 148)

The allocation of the funds that are meant for the upliftment of the poor are mismanaged by the office bearers of the village administrative units who would make sure the money remains in their control while the Dalits languish as borrowers as their loan money multiplies through the years, and they continue to be subservient to the upper class. The Svarna class would help them and pose to be their saviours whereas, in reality, they are the real cause of their miseries. This convention has continued for centuries making it impossible for the feudalistic system to come to an end and allowing the traditional hierarchical model to crumble. The following lines would help in understanding the above lines in a better way.

> All the money meant for the welfare of the Dalits would be appropriated by these influential people. Thus, Dalit upliftment would be carried out on paper and the Dalits would never know anything about it. And in a year or two when they received recovery notices from banks, they would be shocked and go to the pradhan or the landlords who would lend them money to pay off the loans. Thus, the debtors would remain debtors and the tiny amounts thus borrowed would pile up to thousands without the knowledge of the borrowers. (Harnot 151)

Though the protagonist was successful in accomplishing his project of bringing the roads to the village on his own, with the help of the other villagers, the following lines speak volumes about the mindset of the people that would take time to change. The priest is extremely happy with the feat that Som has achieved and wished that his daughter could marry Som. Som was a potential bridegroom for the priest's daughter in his own eyes, but it was the caste difference that makes him give up the thought or rather wish that Som should have been a brahmin to be perfectly eligible for the match. He embraced Som. For a moment he wished that Som belonged to his caste, and then he would have wed his daughter to him.

In the story "Saddle", a very interesting incident is seen where the Dalit is transformed into a Brahmin just for a day to make him a scapegoat for a particular ceremony that requires only a Brahmin to perform it. Since the ceremony involved a high risk to the life of the person performing it, a Dalit man is chosen and converted into a Brahmin only for a day. It is quite ironic that once converted, the conversion is made valid only for the period of the ceremony. If the person survives, even then the moment he gets out of the carrier in which he sits to slip down on a rope, he is a Dalit again! This strange social phenomenon is quite hypocritical. The lines below allow us to understand deeply the concepts of being impure and getting rid of the years-long impurities through a religious ceremony of conversion that made the protagonist Sahaj Ram a sacred Brahmin.

> Sahajram was no longer a Dalit. He bathed in cold water and then underwent all the necessary rituals and ceremonies for his initiation into brahminhood. After these rituals, he was symbolically cleansed of his low caste impurities and transformed into a holy brahmin. People had visions of their deity in him. Otherwise, an untouchable, Sahju was now a brahmin. (Harnot 77)

The Dalit families had long suffered as they were asked to leave their home and village and wander about in search of new land and food, years ago. They had settled at a new place to start a new life, moving on with times. However, the wounds of the past were still fresh in the minds of the older men who had been witness to this harassment and ordeal of losing their family members. Now, the same village people had come to the doorsteps of these once outcasted people as they were in dire need of a person who would agree to be the Brahmin for a day for the ceremony. This depicts the opportunism of the high caste people who are always ready to reap benefits at the behest of the Dalits but never allow them to come at par with them socially and economically. They were helped by a family who had given them a piece of land to build their huts on a small hamlet, far away from their ancestral village. The following lines portray the condition of the Dalit families who were ousted from their ancestral village.

> When long ago, the Dalit families were forced to leave the village, they wandered about for many days, looking for food and shelter. Many of them died. With much difficulty, they approached a family which helped them with a piece of land on which the expelled families raised their huts, and thus a small hamlet of poor Dalit families came into existence far away from their ancestral homes. (Harnot 83)

The Dalits continue to be marginalised in the villages where they are barred from entering any religious places. The mukhya devta's temple compound was still out of bounds for Dalits. The deplorable condition of the Dalits is depicted vividly in the story when Sehejram sits on the carrier that would be pushed and slid on the rope from the top of the mountain, crossing over the deep gorge to reach the base of the hill. This is also symbolic of the fall of a Dalit as a Brahmin from the top of the mountain at the beginning of the ceremony to that of the original status as a wretched Dalit at the end of the ceremony provided he survives the risk of his life. He could see his fellowmen standing on one nook of the ground where they had assembled.

> Now Sahju's eyes turned towards the Dalits standing in one corner of the ground. The maximum voices of exaltation were coming from that direction. Their hearts were clean and unblemished. Their voices were untainted by any selfishness. Their clothes were tattered. There were women whose breasts showed through their torn and ragged kurtas. Their hair was uncombed. Instead of coloured ribbons, there were pieces of grass and dried leaves entangled in their hair. Their children were also with them who had naked legs and bodies or were dressed only in tattered shirts. There were blisters on their feet and unfathomable pain in their eyes. (Harnot 96)

CHAPTER 7

Resisting Caste Hierarchies through Education

People who have been marginalised are no longer silent spectators to the behavior meted out to them. They show defiance and retaliation against any kind of disparity that they experience at the hands of the higher caste people. The stories of SR Harnot have presented the characters who have stood up and spoken against the discrimination practiced by the society based on the caste of the people. Here is an attempt to analyse the characters and incidents where they manage to not only express their displeasure but also assert their rights.

In the story, 'The Saddle', the way Sahaj Ram spoke suggested that he was not illiterate. He was well aware of his rights in the modern world while also being able to understand the opportunistic nature of the high caste people who had approached them for the culmination of their selfish interests. Sahaj Ram was candid enough to ask these questions from the people who had approached him to be upgraded as a brahmin only for one day for the ceremony.

> Why is it that an untouchable is worshipped as a brahmin only for the duration of the ceremonies? And suppose an accident happened and her husband died, then which of the devtas, in whose honour numerous goats and lambs have been slaughtered, would bring him back to life? (Harnot 92)

However, after the ceremony, when he lands safely on the ground, after putting his life at risk, Sahaj Ram makes sure that before he is relegated to his caste again, he makes the most of the opportunity that he has been provided with to ensure that the rights of his community are restored. The land and the homes that his ancestors were asked to leave and go may be returned to his people while he still sat on the seat that was made for him. He knew that his voice could be heard only till the time he sat on the seat, the moment he gets down, he won't be heard nor his needs catered to. This shows how the subalterns in the story want to defy the long-standing traditions that have always kept them marginalised in society.

> Do you know, Sharma Ji, I am the greatest pandit at this moment, the most precious deity, everybody's object of reverence. But as soon as I come down, I will be the same old untouchable and you will all become upper caste brahmins, and thanks again. The priests and brahmins who today are standing before me with folded hands and beseeching eyes will tomorrow run away … "Then return our lands, Sharma Ji. We want to settle here, in this very village from where your ancestors had chased us away." This was an unexpected blow. Sharma Ji wasn't prepared for it. He felt as if he was going to faint. A passing thought came to him that he should teach an appropriate lesson to this low-caste scum of the earth right now and tell him how he should talk to his superiors. But the occasion demanded that he swallow this bitterness. He was sweating and wiped the sweat drops off his forehead repeatedly. That Sahju would turn the tables on him and that too on an occasion like this, had never occurred to him even in his wildest imagination. But today this beda can say and do anything without any let or hindrance. He could ask for anything. Sharma Ji turned to the temple committee members and the priest as if seeking their advice. They all agreed that nothing could be refused to Sahju today. Sharma ji had to say yes and he said it. Sahju knew that any gift, whether in cash or kind, given to him today could not be taken back. He gently pushed the grass saddle on the rope and slid it down to the ground. The crowd burst out with joy and gave shouts of jubilation. Sacred music was sounded all around and it filled the air. The atmosphere was now charged with devotion and holiness (Harnot 97)

The whole ceremony was arranged by Sharma Ji who wanted to take the credit for organising this event after so many years. This also would have marked the beginning of his political career after he had retired from government service. The Dalits were used for their purpose by convincing and persuading them to be a part of the ceremony as they were an indispensable part of the same. However, it never occurred to them that Sahaj Ram would put such a demand in front of them in the guise of the Brahmin who could not be denied anything that day. Their plan was ruined and they were caught in a situation in which they could not refuse Sahaj Ram for the favour that he had asked for. It was a matter of their right and justice for them. "They knew that they could not turn away from their promise as that would invite calamity to the whole village but despite this fact, they could not reconcile to the situation of bending before the Dalits." (Harnot 98) In this manner, Sahaj Ram ensures that the risk that he had taken for his life should not go in vain. He makes sure that not only were the lands and the homes returned to the people of his community but also that the promises made to them be fulfilled in the presence of the huge crowds that had gathered to witness the feat. Sahaj Ram was a brahmin that day and not listening to him would hurt the sentiments of the villagers who would take it as a bad omen that could invite misfortune to the village and the people. This was a masterstroke by Sahaj Ram who didn't budge from the seat unless the demands were agreed upon. He knows that he could exercise some powers that day as an empowered Brahmin and uses his position for the upliftment of his community.

In the next story, Svarna Devta Dalit Devta, the protagonist is well aware of the fact that he is better than the students belonging to the high caste in school. Though not encouraged to study further either by his parents or the by the other people in the society, he raises his voice against this injustice. Poverty was one reason which forced the students of his caste to quit their studies and help their parents in earning a livelihood to sustain themselves. However, the protagonist doesn't accept it easily and questions the tradition that has been followed by the earlier generations.

> Another reason might have been the pressure of my caste people in the village but the reason for poverty was real and I understood it quite well. I was the first-ever Dalit student to have passed the class eight examination and it was a matter of pride as well as jealousy for the Dalits of my village and the surrounding ones. I had also stood first in the whole district while many savarna students had failed. (Harnot 113)

Besides the discrimination in the imparting of education, there were many other social norms where they faced the insensitivity of the higher caste. One such incidence has been narrated in the story, where the protagonist and his community are subjected to such inhuman behaviour that they are made to sleep in the open with no proper arrangements of bedding and warm blankets. The biting cold is too much for the protagonist and his people but they don't raise their voices or demand anything from the host family. Whereas the higher caste people sleep cozily, covered in warm and thick quilts just a few feet away from the musicians maintaining distance. However, the protagonist decides to pull away from one of the two quilts that the priest had taken over himself while the people were suffering outside in the cold. This action of the protagonist depicts how the new generation was not ready to accept the harsh behaviour meted out to them. They don't hesitate to assert their rights and are willing to snatch them away if they are deprived of the same.

> We looked around but nothing was to come our way. My fellow musicians covered themselves with their torn and tattered cotton shawls

> and fell asleep. I also thought of somehow spending the night in the open but found it difficult to control my anger. A priest was sleeping near the chariot wheels and had covered himself with two heavy quilts. I pulled one quilt but this disturbed the priest's sleep and he woke up. Initially, he couldn't make out what had happened but when he saw me holding the quilt, he scowled and began to shout obscenities at me. This awakened the others and they got up as if buckets of freezing water had been poured on them. There was a huge commotion now and all eyes turned to me. (Harnot 118)

However, this was taken as a direct challenge to the superior position of the higher caste people who made a big hue and cry of this incident. This act of defiance was made out to be a big issue and was related to the education of the new generation. The pundits saw this as the consequence of the education that the boys of the lower caste had started to gain. They think that it's due to the new education system that the Dalits equate themselves with the traditional brahmins who were the respected people of the community. Snatching away the quilt of a Brahmin while he was asleep was an act that depicts the degradation of the values that the people have been imbibing for generations. The brahmins tried to counter this uprising against them very aggressively to make sure that no one else dares to do this again. Such acts of defiance had to be suppressed or it would amount to bigger revolts from the lower caste people. The protagonist narrates the incident in the story:

> He turned on me like a ferocious dog and shouted, "A little bit of education seems to have gone to the heads of these low caste people and swelled their pride. How could you snatch the quilt of a pious brahmin? And what will I do with this now that you have touched it with your filthy hands? (Harnot 118)

The protagonist's hands were taken to be 'dirty' as the Brahmin raised his voice and even tried to assault him with his hands when his hands were met with strong resistance. The confrontation resulted in bigger chaos as the Brahmin fell owing to his force that was reverted by the protagonist. The Brahmin fell on the pole on which the tent had rested, pulling the whole of it down. However, the speaker didn't budge from his position even as the brahmins hurled abuses at them but made sure that they didn't hit him. The speaker taking advantage of this commotion, asks the host Leeladas as to why they were treated in such an inhuman manner not being provided with warm bedding on this freezing night. These musicians were the ones who had made the jataras a success but ironically, they are out to cast and made to suffer miserably. This speaks volumes about the degree of resistance that the protagonist had put up against the discrimination that they had faced. They were now not ready to accept the illogical traditions of keeping the so-called untouchables at a distance that stood irrelevant in today's scenario. The author narrates:

> He raised his hand to hit me but I held it before it could touch me. He was so taken aback by my resistance that he collapsed and fell on one of the bamboo poles that had been fixed to support the tarpaulin, with the result that a portion of it fell on him. Nobody had foreseen those things would take such an ugly turn and lead to a physical scuffle. The brahmins took it as an affront to their honour but, even though abuses continued to flow unabated, they held themselves back from advancing toward me. The shower of abuses made it difficult for me to restrain myself any longer. I moved towards Leeladas who was standing at some distance from me and said, "Pandit, so far, I have remained patient and borne with the abuses which are being showered on me but I wish to seek an answer from all you brahmins who are here to earn merit by participating in this holy occasion: do only brahmins feel the fury of this freezing night or kolis and chamars also? All of you have been comfortably snoring under two quilts each but for us, you have not arranged even dry rice stalks or grass. Don't you feel that we are also human beings and feel cold or heat as you people do? Our priests and panchs may not feel ashamed but Pandit Leeladas, you organised this occasion, you are the host and we came because you had invited us. You have organised the jataras, not of just one deity but three deities and you should have known that there would be not only brahmins but people of other castes also and they would need to be provided with quilts and blankets. (Harnot 118)

This incident was a new beginning for the Dalits and encouraged the protagonist to take a stance against the prejudiced behaviour of the upper caste people. He was now ready to take further steps against the social setup and the existing norms. The next morning was an awakening in a way that the protagonist had experienced. This morning he decided what he had to do to make the Dalit devtas look as affluent as the Svarna devtas. The following lines from the story would throw more light on the same: –

> The next morning, I woke up early and opened my trunk. Last week my father bought a suit-piece for me. Silently I took it out, held it under my arms, and ran towards the temple. I was panting when I reached there. Nobody had seen me on the way. I looked around, took off my shoes, crossed the boundary wall, and sat down at the feet of the statue of the dwarpal. I touched his feet, unfolded the suit-piece, and wrapped him in it from head to foot. Pleased, I came out of the temple and wore my shoes. Initially, I thought of going back through the usual narrow track but then my heart said today; why not take the path that passes right through the brahmin houses. (Harnot 128)

These lines show how the defiance was resisted strongly by the brahmins and countered back equally by the protagonist who was determined to demand equal rights not only for himself but also for his Dalit devtas who were made to stand out to face the climatic furies. The incident makes him bolder as he not only covers the Dalit Devta with rich clothes as were worn by the Svarna Devtas but also decides to take the forbidden path that crossed through the brahmin locality and was used only by the upper castes. The narrow road that he trod on since his childhood is also symbolic of his narrow vision and scope in life that he wishes to broaden with time to change his fate. In the story 'In the Name of Gods', Som is the protagonist who belongs to the lower caste. He too like the character in the previous story undertakes all the geographical hardships and social challenges to pursue his education. He manages to score better than the other students of his village who hailed from the upper castes. This ability to rise from the deplorable conditions that his forefathers lived, in depicts the strong will of the younger generation who are determined to alter their destiny with the help of education.

> Som in realising his ambition to pass the high school. In the first year, Som would start for the school quite early in the morning and reach the school on time. He would reach back home very late in the evening. His passion for education had the better of all his fears of the dark and the lonely forest road and the wild animals. He would manage to do the school assignments in the light of the sun someplace on his way back from the school and cram his lessons as he walked home. The total distance that he covered on foot every day was about twenty kilometres but this did not deter him and he passed the high school in the first division. This was news for the whole region because he was the first to have passed the high school and that too in the first division! His father's pride in his son's abilities was beyond words. (Harnot 147)

The father's pride as talked about in the above lines is not only the happiness of Som scoring good marks but also the fact that he crossed all the hurdles to pass with flying colours. It was also the joy that Som eventually succeeds in achieving a feat that the others failed to achieve. This was symbolic of the struggle against the social norms and eventually overcoming the same as Som gets educated. The following lines throw light on the success that Som has achieved by getting employed. This marks an end of the forced professional conventions that the people had been following and were forced to follow. Som was a weaver's son but gets educated to join a government job that is contrary to the expectations of the villagers.

> He had already registered his name in the employment bureau and after a few days, he got a call letter from a government department. He was overjoyed at the prospect of being selected for the post of clerk. He informed his parents immediately for whom the news was a real god-send. But it didn't go down well with the so-called big people of the village who were not prepared to believe that a weaver's son would succeed where their own sons had failed. (Harnot 147)

The big people refer to the upper caste, a rich and influential lot who couldn't digest the fact that Som has not only gained an education and scored better marks than their children but also that he has been selected for a government job. This is like a bolt from the blue for these people. It is a beginning of a new era that would ensure equality among all. However, this doesn't end here. Som determined that the funds allocated for the developmental works for the upliftment of the people of his community and the poor. On finding out that the money had not been utilised for the purpose for which it was allotted, Som decides to take the initiative, much to the displeasure of the influential people. They felt insecure now that their position would also be shaken as Som was supported by most of the villagers for his work.

> When the village pradhan and his henchmen came to know that the son of the weaver had dared to found an organisation called the Village Development Committee, they were angry and took it as an affront to their authority and prestige. They simply couldn't digest the fact that somebody else should take the initiative of developing the village while they were still around. They took it as an open challenge to their hold over the village. (Harnot 149)

The following lines depict that it was due to the education that he had received and the job that he had secured that he was able to discover the development schemes that he decides to follow in a pattern for the village with the help of a few men. "Thus, he had behind him a band of like-minded persons who were interested in the development of the village. Due to their jobs, they had become acquainted with new models of development and were keen to replicate those models..." (150). On the completion of his developmental projects, a ceremony is arranged which is attended by the whole village, irrespective of caste. There is no segregation and all are treated as one. As is evident from the following lines from the story, Som was happy to have envisioned such an image that would allow people belonging to all castes to come together on the same platform. It was an idea of a utopian society that he had imagined and had succeeded in creating.

> There was no community, no brahmin, no kanat, no lohar, just one whole village. Only the pradhan and his henchmen were indifferent and kept themselves aloof from the ceremony. There was more bitterness and anger in their hearts than joy and enthusiasm in the hearts of all the people. The success of the committee did not go down well with them at all. They could neither accept it nor show their resentment. (Harnot 161)

Conclusion

Therefore, Harnot is a pioneer of Dalit literature depicting the intricacies of the caste hierarchies that exist in the society of the mountains in his writings. The chapter encapsulates the features and the resistance posed by the educated lower class. This chapter has earnestly tried to capture the changing trends in the society which has led to the Dalits emerging stronger due to the education that they receive, whether it be a pipe player or a Dalit turned into a brahmin for a day. The modern education system helps the downtrodden and poor people hailing from the lower castes to live to pursue the livelihood that they dream about instead of following the age-old traditional practices. The rise of these subalterns has played a pivotal role in shaping their destiny and recreating a world that is free from all the flaws of the caste system. The chapter tries to depict the age-old practices of sidelining and marginalising the Dalits by the upper castes. The different communities like the pipe players, weavers, and other lower caste who had been made scapegoats for performing the religious ceremonies and their characteristics have been portrayed. The social distinctions that had been created and the customs that segregated the lower castes from the mainstream of the society for the fear of being polluted have been thrown light upon. Awakening brought in by education and the discontinuing ancestral professions by the new generation creates chaos and stir in society. This is a direct challenge to the canonical authority and the strict hierarchy followed by the higher castes leading to conflicts between the defiant and educated new generation and the higher caste. The chapter tried to capture the protesting features that are depicted by the author in his stories. The developmental activities that take place in the villages are due to the efforts of the newly educated lower castes who have been provided with the opportunity to hold positions of power and authority. This enables them to utilise the funds meant for them for the implementation of the policies that have been formed for the upliftment of the subjugated class. In this manner, the resistance is validated by the lower castes, forcing the powerful authoritative groups to acknowledge their presence and grant them their long-pending rights and privileges.

CHAPTER 8

Aesthetics of the Mountains and Ecology

The Chapter looks into the environmental concerns that haunt the hilly areas and threaten to disturb the ecological balance that exists there. Mountains have been an abode of nature with meandering rivers, snow-capped ranges, clear blue skies, green meadows, and pristine lakes thriving in their laps. The animal kingdom of the hills is no less fascinating and together they create a sustainable ecosystem. In the stories of SR Harnot, the various aspects of the environmental concerns like the impact of constructing dams, water pollution, and forest fires have been dealt with. The narrative in the stories depicts how the attempts are made to maintain balance in the environment by the animal kingdom and by humans who try to restore their faith in the local deity by reaching out and calling for his help, expecting a miracle to happen.

The rise of an environmentally oriented criticism was an outcome of the literary and cultural studies in the 1990s. The stories of SR Harnot let us have a glimpse into the dynamics of the present day which leads to environmental degradation, disturbs the ecological equilibrium, and affects human life causing a large-scale physical as well as emotional and cultural damage. The themes of environmental concerns are analysed in the chapter by using the Ecocriticism theory.

> "Ecocriticism" was a term coined in the late 1970s by combining "criticism" with a shortened form of "ecology" – the science that investigates the interrelations of all forms of plant and animal life with each other and with their physical habitats. "Ecocriticism" (or by alternative names, environmental criticism, and green studies) designates the critical writings that explore the relations between literature and the biological and physical environment, conducted with an acute awareness of the damage being wrought on that environment by human activities. (Abrams 98)

Thus, we can say that Ecocriticism is the study of literature and the environment from an interdisciplinary point of view, where literary scholars analyse texts that illustrate environmental concerns and examine the various ways in which literature treats the subject of nature.

> "Ecocriticism" was a term coined in the late 1970s by combining "criticism" with a shortened form of "ecology" – the science that investigates the interrelations of all forms of plant and animal life with each other and with their physical habitats. "Ecocriticism" (or by alternative names, environmental criticism, and green studies) designates the critical writings that explore the relations between literature and the biological and physical environment, conducted with an acute awareness of the damage being wrought on that environment by human activities. (Abrams 98)

Michael P. Branch traced the word ecocriticism in the essay Literature and Ecology: An Experiment in Ecocriticism written by William Rueckert in 1978. Cheryll Glotfelty working definition in *The Ecocriticism Reader* is that "ecocriticism is the study of the relationship between literature and the physical environment" (Glotfelty xviii). Ecocriticism is a broadway for literary and cultural scholars to investigate the global ecological crisis through the intersection of literature, culture, and the physical environment. Ecocriticism originated as an idea called "literary ecology" which was used as a term by Joseph Meeker and was later coined as "-ism" by Rueckert in 1996. Ecocriticism expanded as a widely used literary and cultural theory by the early 1990s with the formation of the Association for the Study of Literature and Environment (ASLE) at the Western Literary Association in 1992. Later, the journal named *ISLE: Interdisciplinary Studies in Literature and Environment* was launched in 1993. The publication of *The Ecocriticism Reader* by Glotfelty and Fromm in 1996 led to wider use of the term. Karl Kroeber in his book *Romantic Imagining and the Biology of Mind* argues that literary criticism needs to connect to a wide range of social activities rather than just aesthetics. The terms 'ecocriticism' was revived in 1989 by Glotfelty and in 1992 he founded the Association for the Study of Literature and Environment (ASLE). He along with Harold Fromm edited a collection of essays *The Ecocriticism Reader: Landmarks in Literary Ecology* in 1996 which led to wider use of the term Ecocriticism.

SR Harnot has depicted a more primitive and less urbanised form of an environment that is free of the pollutants from cities and towns. The stories depict a life that is still enveloped by the natural environs. Lawrence Buell writes "… "pastoral" has become almost synonymous with the idea of (re)turn to a less urbanised, more "natural" state of existence" (Buell, 31). The two stories that have been taken up from the translated stories of SR Harnot are "The River has Vanished" and "Aabhi". This may be called the green reading of the place where the author belongs to. An extensive imagery of the landscape has been illumined by the author in these stories specifically that helps in the creation of the ecological backdrop to these narratives which tell a very important tale. As is explained by MH Abrams, the analysis of such texts leads to a better interpretation of the environment and ecology of the place.

> Many ecocritics recommend, and themselves exemplify, the extension of "green reading" (that is, analysis of the implications of a text for environmental concerns and toward political action) to all literary genres, including prose fiction and poetry, and also to writings in the natural and social sciences. Within the literary domain, the endeavor is to elevate the status or to include within the major canon of literature, the hitherto undervalued forms of nature writing and of local color or regional fiction by authors such as Thomas Hardy, Mark Twain, and Sarah Orne Jewett. (Abrams 100)

Literary ecology explores the relationship between literature and the physical environment, reflecting our relationship and interactions with the physical world. Nature and literature have always been depicted in the works of poets and writers in almost all cultures of the world across the ages. This intimate relationship between the natural and social world is being analysed and emphasised in all the faculties of higher education and research. The literary critic tries to study how this has been textualised by the writers in their works. In this context, two terms have become very important today – ecology and ecocriticism. India is a country with a variety of ecosystems that range from the Himalayas and the Great Plains in the north to plateaus and beaches in the south and from the Sunderbans in the east to the Thar Desert in the west. However, these ecosystems have been adversely affected and literature could not remain unaffected and aloof from this phenomenon.

Tradition and Aesthetic

The beauty of nature and the environment is demonstrated vividly in the stories of SR Harnot. The natural environs form the basis of the narratives that depict the livelihood of the folks of the hills and their lives are intermingled with nature as naturally as fish to water. People thrive on the natural environment, depending on them from the basic necessities of food, clothing, and shelter to the other needs that are catered for by the trees and the animals. The very existence of people thrives and prospers in their natural environs. The narratives in the story allow one to have a deeper look into the aesthetics of the hills and depict a life that is still organically simple. The aesthetics form an important essence in the stories where the elements of nature are fairly described using words supplemented by a description of the lifestyles that are harmoniously balanced with the environment.

> In his Latin treatise entitled Aesthetica (1750), the German philosopher Alexander Baumgarten applied the term "aesthetica" to the arts, of which "the aesthetic end is the perfection of sensuous cognition, as such; this is beauty." In present usage, aesthetics (from the Greek, "pertaining to sense perception") designates the systematic study of all the fine arts, as well as of the nature of beauty in any object, whether natural or artificial. (Abrams 5)

The aesthetics of the mountains and hills with the rivers and lakes have been depicted by SR Harnot vividly in the stories. The stories throw light upon an ecosystem that is sustained by the interrelationship between nature, people, and the animals living in that environment.

> Ecocriticism has come to mean not only the application of ecology and ecological principles to the study of literature, but also the theoretical approach to the interrelational web of natural cultural and supernatural phenomena. It began to explore constructions of environment in literary texts and theoretical discourse. Since literature has always conditioned our philosophical understanding of nature, of environment. Even the aesthetic categories by which our feelings for nature are understood the beautiful, the picturesque, the scenic, the sublime, the wild etc. have been defined largely by their use in literary and critical contexts. (Shikha 3)

The beauty of nature is depicted in a symbolic form as in the story the mood of the characters and the incidents corresponds with the progression of the story. RK Narayan, whose novels and short stories have a specific region as a backdrop, has exploited the entire social, psychological and regional atmosphere in his writing using nature as the setting and background in his novels and short stories. Nature plays both positive and negative roles. The flowing Saryu River in *The Guide* and the depiction of nature in Malgudi are fine examples of the aesthetics of nature.

Raja Rao has also applied/invoked Nature and nature elements for expressing mythological, regional, and social views. His famous novel, *Kanthapura* depicts the South Indian customs, culture, and environment realistically. He has portrayed the co-relation between mankind and Nature and projects the role and importance of Nature beautifully in human life. Through the depiction of rivers, mountains, and other natural elements, he has depicted this co-relationship with the villagers. The Stories of SR Harnot can also be viewed in the same light as Nature forms an integral part of the people of this beautiful hilly state. As Khemraj and Meenakshi Paul explain his writings in the Introduction to the *Cats Talk*:

> Harnot's flair for photography equips him with an eye for detail and mounting a scene with deft touches of contrast, interest points, and perspective. His description of action and events is almost cinematic and he draws nature's vignettes with the painter's palette. He writes in a deceptively simple and lucid language that allows for an in-depth unfolding of human nature. (Harnot 3)

The following lines express the beauty of the mountains vividly, allowing us to have a glimpse of the views of the mountainous regions. The narrative allows us to speculate on the exquisite and radiant comeliness as Harnot portrays organically in the following lines:

> The rainy season had just started. It was about seven in the morning. By this time, despite the sun still being behind the mountains in the east, its glow could be seen everywhere lying like a golden sheet over the village. But today black clouds covered the mountains. The mountains looked as if they were a part of the sky. Over the mountains in the northern corner of the sky, clouds with frightening shapes could be seen. When the wind scattered the clouds in the east the redness of the morning became visible, making the clouds look as if they were on fire. (Harnot 168)

The mountainous regions witness heavy downpours and showers during the monsoon season which lasts for almost two to three months. The climatic conditions become very challenging during this time affecting the people of this region. However, nature manifests its different wonderful forms and colours in the sky that are overcast with black and grey clouds. Seldom do the Sun's rays show up, creating a beautiful canvas in the sky over the newly bathed mountains. Harnot has illustrated these views through his writings.

> It was then that a number of explosions were heard in the distance, startling the people gathered in the courtyard. They were not clear whether the sound was that of thunder, or of something else. The glass window panes of many houses had cracked. The sound of the lowing and bleating of the cattle, sheep, and goats could be heard from the cattle shed. (1Harnot 68)

The bleating of the animals is a clear indication of the forthcoming environmental dangers that the people are about to face.

Animals have been close associates of the people in the hills, whose lives depend on the cattle in more than one way. Indian writers in English have often portrayed the relationship with the animals in the Indian context quite effectively, creating an amalgam of a plethora of natural surroundings and their impact on human beings. The tribes of India still sustain nature completely and even their faith system incorporates the Sun and Moon as the principal Gods.

> Kamala Markandaya is one of the greatest Indian novelists in English. Markandaya has also used Nature and natural elements for her effective and flawless expressions and descriptions of views. She considers nature as a wild animal. She thinks nature is a destroyer and a preserver both. (Lata 426)

There are more examples of how the writers use nature as a means to convey the impending dangers and relate the seasons with the twists and turns in fictional situations faced by the characters. A village is a social unit that is interdependent on the natural environment including birds and animals. We can find more examples of writers portraying the psychological impact that animals and birds have on the characters and their lives. The animals' behavioral patterns influence human beings forcing them to emulate the same in their lives, also teaching great lessons of companionship that humans have failed in. One such example has been talked about by Kumari Shikha in the following lines.

> Anita Desai is a very prominent and popular woman Indian novelist in English. Nature which includes animals, plants, and birds, has a strong presence in almost all her works. Known in Indian-English fiction for ushering in the psychological novel, Desai uses external landscapes to portray interior states of mind. In Cry the Peacock, the complexities of Maya's inner life is effectively brought out through the landscape as is her resentment against her husband for his inability to communicate with her. (Shikha 4)

The timelessness and the agelessness of mountains and rivers depict the magnificence and the magnitude of their presence on earth and the lives of human beings. Since times immemorial they have stood there and witnessed events taking place through the ages. "The high mountains from which the river started were always covered with glaciers. Some of the blocks of ice on the mountain were even centuries old. The small river was the source of livelihood for the people of many villages." (Harnot 169)

Along with the natural ecosystem, the Local deities have also become an integral part of the people residing in the villages in the hills. Every action of the villagers is accountable to the deity with whom they communicate via the special person known as a 'Chela' who is bestowed with the special powers that allow him to strike a conversation with the villagers. Even the well-educated and the powerful class have to bow in front of the Deity known as the 'devta' in the village to seek his blessing before pursuing anything auspicious. The Deity is the part of the aesthetics of the folk men of the hills.

> It was the priest who suggested that they should seek the blessings of the deity. In any case, the deity of that village was known far and wide for his divine power. So much so that before elections, even the chief minister never forgot to bow before the deity. (Harnot 172)

The interdependence of the animal kingdom is illustrated by the writer in the story 'Aabhi' which is a bird that is known to be a preserver of the sacred lake that has been kept impeccably clean by picking up every little speck of dirt or filth that falls on the surface of the lake waters. The writer throws light on the routine of the bird from dawn till dusk, keeping an eye on the lake and its surroundings.

> Aabhi has been busy for ages. Eons have passed but her work is still not over. Instead, it has only increased in the twenty-first century. She wakes up before sunrise and sits on a rock beside the lake. She dips again and again into the water and flutters her little silken wings. After finishing her bath, she sits singing for a while. The sweet music of her song descends somewhere deep into the pure azure waters of the lake and frolics in the ripples, as if trying to awaken the sleeping lake. Aabhi feels the lake stir languidly from its deep sleep. Then she flies to the threshold of the ancient temple at the bank of the lake. She pecks at the door and sings as if to wake Budhi Nagin Ma reposing inside. Her melodious music permeates the entire jungle. The other aabhis and birds also join her in the dawn chorus. (Harnot 176)

The following extract from Leo Tolstoy's story "Kholstomir" and the extract from "Aabhi" is an elaborated description of the animals living in the jungle and their behavioral pattern with their offspring whom they rear in the most pristine natural environments. It requires a great amount of keen observation and sensitivity to express the same in their writings by the authors. These extracts are a fine example of the aesthetics of the animal kingdom illustrated by the writers in their respective stories. The rare activity is captured by the imagination of the writer, who has symbolically used the process of the shedding of the coat by the female wolf as leaving the old times behind and depicted the wolf cubs gathering around her, representing the new age.

> At dawn, in a ravine of the old forest, down in an overgrown glade, big-headed wolf cubs were howling joyfully. A lean old wolf who was shedding her coat, dragging her full belly with its hanging dugs along the ground, came out of the bushes and sat down in front of the cubs. The cubs came and stood around her in a semi-circle. She went up to the smallest, and bending her knee and holding her muzzle down, made some convulsive movements, and opening her large sharp-toothed jaws disgorged a large piece of horseflesh. The little one, growling as if in anger, pulled the horseflesh under him and began to gorge. In the same way, the mother wolf coughed up a piece for the second, the third, and all five of them, and then lay down in front of them to rest. (Tolstoy 381)

Something similar has been expressed by Harnot in the story where the mother bear with her cubs comes down the frozen lake during the winters to roam around the hard frozen surface of the frozen lake. The winters depict the end of a seasonal year but the cubs hovering around her are symbolic of the new beginning that nature would witness soon in the form of spring season. The interdependence of the animals and birds has also been described as Aabhi sitting on the antlers and enjoying the ride, the musk deers arriving after the leopards have left and there is no danger, and the bear and her cubs who leisurely keep lying down on the snow.

> Aabhi has seen snow leopards and their cubs turn it into their playground. Once the leopards leave, the musk deer and tahr crisscross the frozen lake in rows. At times, she has also spied a swamp deer with long antlers running across the surface with its mates. Aabhi loves to perch quietly on its antlers. The bears are cheerfully content. A mother bear comes along with her little soft cubs and lies down for hours on the frozen lake. The little cubs never tire of romping on the lake. (Harnot 177)

Melting of snow at the onset of the warmer season is a splendid sight and has been described wonderfully as a transformation process from the frozen to the melted form. As a result of global warming, this phenomenon has been captured by the explorers in the north and south poles of the earth where the snowline has been receding and huge icebergs melting and falling on the ocean surface. Trees are bowed down by the weight of the snow over them during the whole winter season, allowing them to come to their original positions as the temperature increases. The regular work is resumed when Aabhi knows that snow has finally melted on the roads as the noise of the vehicles and the ringing of the temple bells confirm that humans are now able to reach the temple doors. The cleaning assignment that Aabhi is bestowed with is mainly the result of the pollution caused by the humans who visit the temple and the dried leaves and twigs of the trees.

> When the snow melts, the frozen layers on the lake begin to split open. It seems to Aabhi as though the lake is trying to make its presence felt from beneath those stretched swathes. The lake has woken from a deep slumber. The frozen white sheet of snow gathers slowly and slips off it. Glass-like frozen pieces of ice begin to float on its surface. Aabhi perches on one and experiences extreme bliss. For long, she sings and glides on the surface of the lake. Deodars, baan oaks, and rhododendrons too lift their heads towards the sky as if thanking God after finishing their penance. Then one morning, when the temple bells ring out or the piercing horn of a vehicle on the road reaches Aabhi's ears, she gets all set to take charge of her work. (Harnot 178)

This was the description of the environmental aesthetics as explained by the author vividly.

CHAPTER 9

Nature-Human Interface: Critiquing Environmental Degeneration and Evaluating Traditional Response in the Himalayas

The global environmental crisis is another aspect that is depicted in the stories by SR Harnot in the context of the hilly state. The construction of dams which is also known as the 'damage', has affected the ecology and the ecosystem of the mountains. The reservoirs formed due to the construction of these dams have created multiple problems in the topography of the hills, drowning the mountains and causing water soaking hence making them weaker through the years.

This is an instance of how nature overpowers man and its designs eventually, paving way for its growth and sustainability. The plans of human beings to derive maximum benefits from nature according to their own need and greed leads to a complete breakdown of the artificial environment that has been manufactured by men. Nature has always proved to be stronger than man. It has often shown its power by controlling manpower through natural calamities like famine, drought, flood, earthquakes etc. Man's life and nature are so interlinked that it is not possible for human beings to separate themselves from its influence. Therefore, they have no choice but to accept both nature's bounty and adversity. This can be said to be reciprocal as nature too is the recipient of man's action. Our irresponsible actions cause irreparable damage to nature. This is how the chain of ecosystems works in which everything is related to each other and therefore affects each other.

Constructing dams has led to the complete depletion of natural resources, changing the properties of the natural elements by converting the free flow of the waters into stagnancy. The construction of dams further leads to the change in the course of the river as well, which has a deeper impact resulting in the vanishing of the river and shifting of the river bed. This incident has been written about in the story "The River Has Vanished". "Teekam ran up panting to the edge of the field below the house and cried, "Pita! Dada! Tau! Come out. The river has vanished." (Harnot 168). The vanishing of a river is a very rare phenomenon that people had never witnessed earlier in their lives. These further impact human lives which are dependent on the river for more than one reason. The daily needs are catered to by the water of the river for irrigation and household activities. The one reference made in the story is about the small water mills in the village that harness the water current to run them for grinding the wheat grains to make wheat flour. However, with the river changing its course or the water stopped from flowing forward, the river bed has turned dry, rendering the water mill useless. As the protagonists say in the story' "Like every day, I reached the gharat on the river bank... went down to turn the kuhal to start the mill, but I saw that there was no water in it." (Harnot 169) To investigate the cause of this snag, when Teekam goes ahead, he was rather shocked to see what had happened to the river. "...When I reached there, I was confused. I could not understand why the river that is never without water had gone completely dry. …The river had really vanished. Its water had dried up." (Harnot 169)

The stakeholders of these multipurpose hydroelectric projects that these dams have come to be known as, try to pacify the villagers who were shocked to see the dry river. The villagers are convinced that the river has not vanished but has been transformed into electricity that would light up their homes and also provide employment to their families and lead to prosperity. Pujari Ji, it is not necessary to get so worked up early in the morning. Your river hasn't gone anywhere. Now it has turned into electricity. It will shine in the region as electric lights. It will bring new jobs for you." (Harnot 170), says the Pradhan (Headman) who is the headman of the village. After the villagers are unable to stop the construction of the dam and their requests fall on deaf ears, the progress of the dam work and its consequences have started being noticed by the people of the village. The water level rises and the lands have begun to sink. The visible effects are elaborated by the writer in these lines. "Now even a road had been constructed passing at a point below their village and because of the digging and the blasting, the hills began to sink. Many acres of land had already sunk. Now their priority was to stop the work." (Harnot 171)

All the negative impacts of the hydroelectric projects have been elaborated on by the writer who has depicted the general mood of the villagers. The village and its surrounding areas would be changed geographically bringing about irreparable damage and transformation for the people. This would also result in a shortage of food and water for the livestock that thrives on the river, with no water for irrigation making it completely dry and barren. The sounds of the river that add to the aesthetics of the mountains would also be replaced by the mechanical noises of the machines.

> A mood of grim sadness pervaded the whole area. There was darkness everywhere. Their village would be consumed by the project. Then there would be no water, neither for their cattle nor for their fields. There would neither be the greenery of the forest nor the sound of the river. There would be nothing left. What would remain would be the thunder of dynamite blasts ... the cracking, collapsing mountains ... the melting glaciers. (Harnot 174)

In the story "Aabhi", the impact of human actions on nature has been narrated in the form of the bird's thought process. People, who visit the lake and the temple as pilgrims, are not aware of the kind of threats that their activities during this visit are posing to nature. The air and noise pollution caused by the vehicle that they are traveling on to reach this place has deeper impacts that are elaborated by the writer in the story.

> The people who come here do not realise for how many long centuries these tiny aabhis have served the lake and Budhi Nagin Ma. They do not know that their actions are destroying the jungles and the hills. They do not know that the noise of their vehicles has destroyed the solitude of the wild animals, and in fear, they crouch in their several caves far away. They do not know that Budhi Nagin Ma's eyes are being blinded by the smoke of diesel and petrol. They do not know that these deodars, deep in penance, are at the final leg of their lives, and at any time they would end their lives and fall to the ground. They do not know that the baan oaks no longer ornament themselves as lushly as before. To them, the flowering of the rhododendrons has no worth. They do not know that the milkmaids no longer come to fill their baskets with rhododendron flowers because they are afraid of falling prey to the savagery of beasts in human form. (Harnot 179)

The environmental pollution caused by the non-biodegradable plastic bottles has littered the surface of the water of the lake. Aabhi keeps the water clean by picking up little twigs and leaves that fall on the water but the plastic trash thrown in the lake is an utter nuisance and toxic for the lake as well as the pristine environment of the forest. "For Aabhi, the plastic trash has become evil. The empty plastic bags and bottles that float on the pure waters of the lake are not fallen leaves or bits of grass. These do not grow on any tree of her jungle." (179) The most dreaded challenge that Aabhi is concerned about, is deforestation. As the region becomes approachable when the snow melts during the summers, the men intrude into the forest and cut the trees. Though this is an illegal activity, these men go about cutting the trees during the night time when no one can notice them. However, the animals and the birds are aware of this deforestation going on but they are helpless, being unable to stop the men. The fury of nature is depicted by the sounds of the howling winds from a distance. Symbolically, the darkness of the jungle, when the trees are cut, is the dark future of these green and dense forests. The teeth of the axes seem to be eating up the forest. This shakes the faith of the bird in God as well who she sees as a silent spectator or absent.

> Aabhi's problems are growing now. It was all right as far as picking up straws and leaves off the lake, but what of the strange men who come into the darkness of the jungle with sweeping lights. The sharp axes and sharp-toothed saws on their shoulders frighten the entire jungle. Trees tremble at the sight of the gleaming axes and the dark evil in the hearts of the barbaric jungle mafia. Winds cower, hidden behind the clouds in silver valleys. It seems that the terrible darkness would destroy the whole jungle. No one is around at that time. God is invisible somewhere in the heavens. (Harnot 179)

Another problem that the writer has attempted to bring to the fore is forest fires that consume the forest drastically leading to mass destruction of the trees. The cause of the forest fires is more man-made than natural. Harnot has tried to explore one cause of the forest fire by illustrating the negligence of men who smoke and throw away their half-lit cigarettes in the forest. This bird is unable to pick these burnt stubs, disturbing the balance of nature. "She goes close and realises that these were not glow worms. These were half-lit butts of cigarettes and biris. She tries to pick up the butts in her beak in the thick darkness but ends up scorching her mouth." (180). Trying to capture the thought of the Budhi Nagin Ma, who is the Goddess of the temple near the lake, the writer explains how even the Goddess feels disdain towards the presence of the pilgrims who have come to seek her blessings. The worship material has been strewn all over the lake and the holy smoke of the incense no longer fills up the air with fragrance but suffocates her. Her only respite is the presence of the aabhis who make sure that the lake remains clean.

> Budhi Nagin Ma is helpless. She feels herself chained by hundreds of shackles. She has begun to dislike the incense smoke and the lamps. Praise and worship of the people vex her. Their prayers and supplications irritate her. She is frightened of the devils hiding inside the minds of her devotees. She has begun to fear the desolations of the night. Nevertheless, she holds on to the hope that her people, the aabhis would never give in. They would never allow the purity of the lake to be lost. They would pick up every speck of straw or leaf and keep it clean. (Harnot 181)

Another issue and concern addressed through the narrative in the story is the poaching and harassing of the wild animals in the forest by human beings. The wild animals are no longer cocooned in the jungle and are now vulnerable to the human beings who visit the temple during the summer months. The intrusion of human beings in the forest leads to interference with the lives of the wild animals of the jungle. Aabhi's fears have been portrayed by the writer in the story where she apprehends how this evil practice poses a great threat to every animal in the forest.

> Aabhi is greatly troubled today. She has witnessed a petrifying incident. Both Budhi Ma's temple and she have seen some people assault a female snow leopard. The deodars have also heard the loud reverberations of this attack. Her companion aabhis too has heard them. The leopards, bears, and musk deers have also heard them. The peacocks, monals, and jujuranas too have heard them. And the valleys and hills have heard them. They are all bewildered and worried like she is. They have woken fearful and terrified. Aabhi is aware that one day or the other this calamity would fall on each one of them. (Harnot 181)

The reason for forest fires has been attributed to human activities. Whether it is farming or for their benefit, the humans show no concern for the fire that breaks into the forest and destroys natural resources besides killing a lot of animals and birds. Their shelters are burnt away and they are forced to migrate to other areas which may include regions inhabited by human beings as well. This further leads to more complicated situations as the wild animals turn into man-eaters and begin to prey upon human lives in the absence of wild animals in these areas. The cause of the forest fire in the story is due to the smoking of tobacco by human beings. The half-burnt stubs of this burnt biris or cigarettes are thrown away in the forest. Due to the summer season, most of the grass on the land is dry, catching fire instantly. The heat during the day also accelerates the forest causing large-scale damage to the trees and animal kingdom. The negligence of human action and their ignorance pose a great danger to the environment in general and animals in particular.

> He now removes a biri and matchbox from his pocket. He is so intoxicated that he cannot light a match despite striking it several times. After a long time, a blue flame spreads on the heap of twigs with a frightening sound. In the flare, his face looks like the burnt stump of an oak. He takes a few quick drags on the biri before tossing the half-burnt stub aside and begins to look for the leopard again. He has barely walked a few steps when he hears a crackling sound. The dry leaves and straw are on fire. (Harnot 182)

Balance

Traditionally, humans have thrived on the environment for ages, adopting new technologies gradually as modernity creeps in. Maintaining a balance between tradition and the modern world is a challenge that the folks of the hills have to face. The ecology of each region and place is dependent on climatic conditions and other factors. Disturbing one can lead to the collapse of the whole system. "Today ecology is defined as the way in which plants, animals, and people are related to each other and their environment. In this relationship, they are so much interdependent on each other that any disturbance in one disturbs the other." (Shikha 1). In the story "The River has Vanished", when all the attempts of the villagers to prevent the construction of the dam fail, they resort to the traditional practice of seeking the blessing of their deity, who is the local devta. This was now a matter of faith that was sensitive and if not complied with would lead to banishment from society. The people feared the wrath of the devta if anything was done without seeking the devta's permission. So much so that even the politicians made sure to seek the devta's blessings that would help them emerge victoriously. "It was the priest who suggested that they should seek the blessings of the deity…the deity of that village was known far and wide for his divine power…even the chief minister never forgot to bow before the deity." (172)

But this time the issue of the hydroelectric project was of utmost importance to the state politics and protest of any kind would not be considered. Though the devta has not agreed to the construction of the dam and the displeasure has also been conveyed to the politicians, the government was in no mood to make any kind of change in the plan. The will of the devta was said to be manipulated by the opposition leaders who didn't want the government to take any credit for these projects. This was a major setback to the people of the village for whom devta's will was supreme.

> When a group of holy men invoked the deity, he was angry. The pradhan, legislator, and the chief minister bore the brunt of his anger. Talk of total destruction was in the air. It was decided that the legislator be called before the deity. An order on behalf of the deity was issued but the legislator did not appear before him. Then an order was sent to the chief minister. In a very balanced tone, the chief minister replied that he had great respect for the deity but to bring the deity in matters of development was some kind of opposition politics. People lost hope. (Harnot 172)

Now people had no other way but to protest in front of the project work that was going on at the site of the proposed dam. This was their way to strike a balance between the modern technological advances and their faith system in the devta. So strong was their belief that they brought the chariot carrying the devta to the site believing that it was now only him who could have come to the rescue of the villagers. This was a convention that the people hoped would keep away the evils of modernity at bay.

> Then they decided that now they would fight the battle together. The work of the company had to be stopped. So, along with the people of that village, people of many other villages too came together and protesting in a large group they stopped the company's work... A conference took place. It was decided to seek the help of the deity. A few people went back and ritually decorated the chariot of the deity in the traditional manner. That was their last option to save their village, river, and their land. (Harnot 172)

Such was the faith that the villagers believed in the supernatural powers of the deity that would provide them protection, and patronage and also help in stopping the company's construction work that was going on at the site of the dam. Though they received no support from any local politician, the devta was considered to be strong enough by them to overcome the work continued by the company. "People had the belief that now no powers that be could crush their protest. They had the deity with them and they had the deity's might with them." (Harnot 172) To overpower the protesting gathering people, police had to resort to canning as directed by their higher authorities. The use of force to curb this uprising was ineffective and people continued to protest against the government and the company, only to be subjected to a harsher form of resistance from the police who had now opened fire upon them leading to a fatal injury of the chariot carrier and the head priest by the bullets. Shaking their confidence and faith, this incident frightened them to the core, leaving them with no other option but to quit their movement and revert. The falling down of the worship plate held in the priest's hands was a bad omen symbolising that their protest was subjugated.

> When lathis proved ineffective on the bodies of those mountain people, grown strong working in mud and dung, guns were taken out. Then suddenly the firing began. The first bullet struck an old custodian of the deity's wrath. He stumbled down the hill. The second bullet hit the main priest. He cried out. The plate of flowers, rice, and vermilion fell from his hand and he collapsed on the ground losing consciousness. People were in a state of panic. Now it was becoming difficult to continue facing the bullets. They began to retreat. They began to run away (Harnot 173)

The impact of modernity and the changing faith of the people were challenges for the people of the hills who still had hopes for their deity whom they considered to be all-powerful. A miracle was what the villagers were expecting to happen to redeem all the wrong that was done.

> The officers of the company had arranged everything for them. In the beginning, the policemen and the company people were surely afraid of the deity. They were afraid of the miracles they had heard performed by him, but now those were merely stories. When the police had fired, that all-powerful deity ran away, carried on the backs of people. (Harnot 174)

Though the deity's power was questioned and doubted by the policemen who managed to chase away the villagers with the use of the force and bullets, they had not expected the events to take an ugly turn the next day itself, blaming them for the unexpected turn of events of which they had no clue. The shaken faith had to be redeemed by the deity as expected by the people who expected the devta to perform a miracle and restore their unflinching faith. It was also a matter of pride for the devotees of that region who were harshly beaten up by the policemen. Their hopes were now pinned on their god who was the indisputable ruler of the region no one could have replaced the deity's position in the hearts and minds of the people.

> But the next day the newspaper headlines broke the news that people who had been the victims of oppression that day had attacked intoxicated policemen and company people who were celebrating their success with meat and drink, and also that in the morning, there was no trace of them left behind. At the scene, lay only some guns, a few lathis, dozens of broken liquor bottles, goats' heads and skin, and some torn pieces of

> khaki uniforms. Perhaps the deity, whom the oppression of the police had turned into a deserter, appeared collectively in the villagers and the anger of the people destroyed the oppressive arm of the government. (Harnot 175)

The above lines point toward the technique of ambiguity that the author has applied as a technique in the text to create a mystery around the events that happened the previous night. The policemen involved in the canning and firing of the villagers were brutally hurt when they were making merry at night. The anger of the villagers was unleashed on the policemen. This is attributed to the deity who bestowed the power on these villagers to avenge their beatings the previous day. This was a sort of miracle of the deity himself, empowering the villagers to seek help for themselves and strike a balance by not letting the evils of modernity spoil their ecosystem. Devta is a symbol of tradition and convention that the villagers still worship and have immense faith in.

In the next story "Aabhi", the birds have been portrayed as the symbols of natural balance that the ecology of the lake has maintained for ages. These birds have been keeping the lake clean and averting any impact of modernity and tourism on this age-old pristine lake. Though the methods that the aabhis have adopted seem to be inadequate in today's times, they still have been successful in keeping it speck free. It is a great team while they perform their duty. However, the amount and quantity of the garbage and trash that is being thrown on the surface of the water had increased rendering the task harder for them with each passing day.

> Many aabhis gather around on hearing her cry. They know why she has called to them. Although they all clean the lake in different places, they know that now they must work together. They fly over the lake in twos and fours. They join their wings together and try to lift the waste. But despite their best efforts, they fail to do so. They sit atop the domes of the temple and begin to chatter. This chattering is not ordinary. It bears their anguish at the pollution of the pristine lake. (Harnot 178)

The problem of hunting and poaching by men also is a great challenge that is to be faced by the birds. They have found their way of defending and made efforts to resist the attempts made by the men to kill the mother leopard in the story. They covered the leopard by bringing small leaves and twigs and placing them on her to camouflage her body with the colours of the jungle, thereby concealing her from the men's view. The duty of the bird has now not been restricted only to keeping the lake immaculately clean but also to being a saviour of the forests and the animals that thrive on it around the lake.

> She agonises over how to save the leopard. How to give a lease of life to the little ones? She braces herself. Opens her beak with great difficulty. Spreads her wings. The rustling of her feathers is the silent voice of her soulful entreaty. Slowly and gradually a number of aabhis gather there. Aabhi takes the lead. She wants to conceal the leopard. She picks up a twig and places it on the leopard. (Harnot 182)

The end of the story reveals the power of nature to sustain itself and overpower the men who try to destroy it in any way. The man, who would be responsible for the forest fire, was engulfed in the same due to his negligence. He was burnt down completely, leaving behind a few burnt pieces of cloth leaving them behind like a trail of his presence. These pieces were thrown all over the water only to be picked up by the Aabhi depicting how sincerely they have got back to their duty of keeping the lake clean.

> Then Aabhi breaks into a song. Her companion aabhis also join her in singing. Deodars, oaks, pines, and rhododendrons begin to stir. Animals emerge from their dens. Birds leave their nests. They all think that it is morn and begin to sing the dawn chorus. Aabhi busies herself picking up the burnt pieces of cloth strewn on the lake. (Harnot 183)

These two stories have illustrated the triumph of the people's beliefs that reign over the rural areas till now. Though modern ways have crept into society, the people are unwilling to accept those changes that would pose any threat to the lives of the people and animals, and birds. The construction of the dam was resisted as it would drown the villages and also render the river dry, making their lands barren and their lives difficult. Similarly, the story of the birds, "Aabhi", is a depiction of the desperate attempt and frantic effort that the aabhis have made to save the forest from the evils of pollution and fires on the one hand lives of the animals on the other. In all cases, it is the human action that is ultimately responsible.

Conclusion

Hence, ecocriticism is an important aspect that needs to be inspected when reading the literature on the mountains and rivers. The above analysis has tried to do as much, firstly depicting the natural aesthetics of the mountainous regions and then elaborating on the challenges that they face with the advent of the modern technological methods that promise to bring progress and prosperity to the hills. However, the damage incurred is much more dangerous bringing along long-term irreversible effects than the economic benefits derived from them. The destruction of the mountains by digging and blasting results in the total collapse of the ecology. The mountains would cease to exist due to drowning and weakening in the waters of the artificial lakes that formed to tap it for producing electricity. The natural habitats of the animal kingdoms would be lost. The impacts of the other challenges like noise, water, and air pollution are mapped as human beings begin to interfere with the pristine environs of the region causing concerns. The element of faith is also analysed in the stories as people turn towards their deities and goddesses to protect them from the impending dangers caused to the environment through the authoritative forces of the government. The tactfulness of the writer in creating and presenting a perfect balance between the religious sentiments and the approved projects for the development of the region is quite evident in the stories. All these aspects have been covered in this chapter that very well define the concerns and conflict between the conventional aesthetics and the contemporary need for economic development in the hilly regions.

CHAPTER 10

Delineating Exploitation of Women and Social Stigma in the Hills

The chapter aims to analyse the feminist aspect in the translated stories of SR Harnot originally written as "Kalikh' in Hindi and translated into English by Khem Raj Sharma and Meenakshi F. Paul as "Slur "and "Daarosh" which was originally written as the same and translated by Meenakshi F. Paul. "Slur" is a story about Shyama, a widow, and how a son born to her years after her husband's death and her naming him as her son's father has become a matter of controversy and dispute with her in-laws. Besides, the villagers also look down upon her in disdain for the sin that she has committed. "Daarosh" is a traditional custom that is prevalent in a particular region of the state of Himachal Pradesh whereby a girl is kidnapped by any boy who wants to marry her, even if against her wishes. His custom is a sheer encroachment upon the liberty of a girl to marry a boy of her choice. Feminist criticism took a long time to come to establish itself as a literary discipline, overcoming many challenges through the years. It forms an integral part of literary criticism, forming an important perspective to analyse any text with a feminist point of view.

As a distinctive and concerted approach to literature, feminist criticism was not inaugurated until late in the 1960s. Behind it, however, lie two centuries of struggle for the recognition of woman's cultural roles and achievements, and women's social and political rights, marked by such books as Mary Wollstonecraft's A Vindication of the Rights of Woman (1792), John Stuart Mill's The Subjection of Women (1869), and the American Margaret Fuller's Woman in the Nineteenth Century (1845). Much of feminist literary criticism continues in our time to be interrelated with the movement by political feminists for social, legal, and cultural freedom and equality. (Abrams123)

Feminist criticism aimed to expose the patriarchal setup of the society and create awareness among the women to understand in the first place that their position is not a privileged one and they had been conditioned to accept their plight as inferior beings and be content with their role in the social hierarchy. The male-dominated society is insensitive to the issues of women and considers their problems to be insignificant. "It is male-centered and – controlled, and is organised and conducted in such a way as to subordinate women to men in all cultural domains: familial, religious, political, economic, social, legal, and artistic." (Abrams 125) He further clarifies how feminism has been dwarfed by the females themselves due to the deliberate conditioning since childhood in their families and society to accept the social norms and hierarchy that places them at the base of the social structure. "Women themselves are taught, in the process of being socialised, to internalise the reigning patriarchal ideology (that is, the conscious and unconscious presuppositions about male superiority), and so are conditioned to derogate their sex and to cooperate in their subordination." (Abrams125)

Social Stigma

Talking about the widows in India, they are referred to as 'Vidhwa' which originated from the Sanskrit word 'Vidh' which means 'to be destitute'. (Verma) This speaks volumes about the society as well as the economic condition of the widows in India who are expected to lead a life bereft of luxuries. Their fates are dependent on their husbands and their lives become a burden on others after their spouse's death. The widows in India have been a subject of intense scrutiny and interest by the foreign researchers of Social Sciences and Psychology especially the widows in Vrindavan who were sent away from their homes after their husband's deaths to live an austere life with many restrictions. However, for the widows who stayed back home, the conditions were not very different and they too had to lead a life following the rules laid down for them by society. "The concept of 'abuse' is very much relative and depends on socio-economic and cultural context. India's mortality rates are found 86 percent higher among widows than among married women of the same age vulnerable to abuse, neglect and high levels of deprivation" (Varma 132)

Further studies have shown that the widows in rural India have been subjected more to exploitation and oppressive renunciation which was forced upon them. There is "limited freedom to remarry, insecure property rights, living arrangement of elderly, social stigma, restricted employment opportunities, and lack of social support." (Niswade)The property rights of the widow are always encroached upon, discouraging her to claim the property of her husband's house and not allowing her access to the property at the very onset of her widowhood. The hostile environment created in her in-law's house makes it difficult for the widow to enjoy her basic rights that are not denied to any other member of the family. The widow gets no financial support to pursue the legal course to claim her property right. Whether the widows could exercise their rights depended on factors like her age, children, the sex and age of her children, the interests of the dead husband's lineage and stance adopted by the widow's parents or brothers. In brief, widows without children faced the most difficulty in exercising their rights. And widows with sons had the least difficulty. But it's important to mention that the rights of widows over the land lasted until their sons mature.

The sexual exploitation of the widows is kept under wraps as it would ruin the reputation of the family as well as the other men of the society. The widows refrain from speaking up against it considering that they are in a way dependent on these men economically and socially.

> In many households, widowed women either have their own separate arrangement for cooking food or prepare food for them(selves) after the food has been prepared for the family. In many parts of the country, shaving the head of the widow is a common practice. All these measures are aimed towards desexualising the woman so that she becomes unappealing to the many prying eyes of near and far male relatives. (Parmar 3)

The women are considered to be 'manhoos' or jinxed as they are held responsible for 'eating' away from their husbands and outliving them. The married women look down upon them and their labour is utilised most effectively by the members of the family in exchange for the meager necessities that they provide her for living a modest life. "The last but not the least mechanism is attributing danger to the widowed woman. She is rendered as a body with an insatiable sexual appetite intending to seduce innocent men and devour them sexually." (Parmar 6) They are banished from society and are alleged to have an evil eye or be possessed by an evil spirit that causes harm to their husbands. This makes her a victim of the wrath of the society which doesn't allow her to lead a life in the mainstream and keeps her segregated from the rest. "They are attributed to supernatural powers and are associated with witchcraft and death." (Parmar 7) This depicts the notion that people usually have regarding the widows who are given different terms to refer to them denoting how marginalised they become after their husband's deaths. They are the subaltern women of the society who suffer emotionally, socially, physically, and economically. The story "Slur" depicts the mental trauma faced by Shyama at the hands of society for bearing a child that no one wants to own. She faces social stigma and is sexually exploited, both of which are further analysed with context to the quoted lines from the story.

The concept of a widowed single mother, Shyama, against the backdrop of her sexual exploitation at the hands of society is explored in this chapter. The issue of naming the father of the child that was born years after the death of the widow's husband creates a stir in the village. The village headman and the other members preside over the discussion on the matter as the whole village was in attendance, intending to slander Shyama to defame and blame her for this illegal child. However, Shyama's shocking disclosures end up exposing the hypocrisy of the village men instead and her family members as well, raising serious questions. The child ultimately inherits the name of his mother in the school register. Shyama's quest for a new feminist identity is accomplished in a way and is socially accepted. The concept of a single mother or single parent is a problem that has been depicted in the story 'Slur' originally written by SR Harnot in Hindi titled 'Kalikh' and translated by Khemraj Sharma and Meenakshi F. Paul in English. It throws light on the plight of a young widow who was sexually exploited by the men of her village in the name of helping her in different ways. The naming of her son who was born years after her husband's death becomes the reason for a social stigma attached to her. The story is analysed from a feminist perspective, looking into how the widow Shyama has been stigmatised for bearing a child whose father's name is unknown. The patriarchal society blames the poor woman for the sin that she has carried in her womb, not realising that she was a passive victim of the sexual exploitation suffered at the hands of the lecherous men of her village. The patriarchal society as is referred to in the Women Studies is elucidated in the Chapter as depicted in the story which portrays the pitiable and pathetic condition of Shyama, exploited and humiliated by the village men and her own relatives. Shyama faced discrimination and humiliation at the hands of the villagers from the time the news of her pregnancy became known to the villagers. She was a widow who had conceived a child years after her husband's death, raising many eyebrows and causing a stir in the village. She was looked down upon by the people as it was considered a sin and a big blot on her character.

> When word spread that Shyama was pregnant, the villagers were filled with curiosity. Whenever she went out or set off to fetch water, both the young and the old watched her closely. Everyone's eyes were drawn to her stomach. Slowly, her belly swelled. The suspicion of the villagers was confirmed. Her in-laws raised a veritable storm. For the people of the village, she was now a fallen woman. (Harnot 137)

Shyama was a mother of a boy called Manu who was an illegitimate child. For the villagers, Shyama's pregnancy was not a matter of grave concern but was an insignificant scandal that may not cause any serious consequences. The women came to the rescue of Shyama during childbirth. "After nine months, when the baby was born, it was a boy. Putting everything aside, the village women had tended to her at the time of delivery." (138). The boy became the center of attraction and a subject of a joke for the villagers who showed no kindness towards this innocent little child. "The child started to grow. People tried constantly to match his face with the youngsters of the village. Everyone had their opinion, but no one could guess the truth. For Shyama's in-laws, the birth of the boy was calamitous." (138)

Manu, Shyama's son, grew up normally in the village until he was admitted to the school where on being asked about his father, Shyama named her deceased husband. This was not acceptable to her father-in-law and other members of her family. The word spread to the whole village and the behaviour of the villagers towards Shyama changed overnight. This was an issue that had challenged the very fabric of the moral values of society. "Shyama's calling out in this way is not new to the villagers. But today it fell on their ears like blasts of dynamite. They all made faces." (130). The matter amplified into a much bigger issue as this would mean legitimatising the child, enabling him to become a claimant of the ancestral property as well. The panchayat was called to settle this controversy which had become the talk of the area around their village too, arousing the interests of everybody. This caused a lot of mental stress and anxiety to Shyama who faced the brunt of being stigmatised all alone unable to garner support from any quarters.

> But Shyama had a son. And this day, the panchayat had been called on account of him … that … Manu is a bastard …! As she recalled this, it seemed as if a pitcher of cold water had been poured on her head. Life began to seep out of her body. She felt deeply embarrassed even in the solitude of her home. (Harnot 131)

Shyama's mental agony was aggravated as she became the focus of the villagers and the topic of gossip for them. She was stared at by the village folk wherever she crossed them. The mysterious and silent response of the villagers to this new development in the village tormented Shyama emotionally. There was a lull in the village that worsened matters for her. A storm was raging in her mind. "It seemed as if a deep silence had settled over the village. If at all Shyama came across any woman, she turned her face away from Shyama; and the men gave a strange laugh when they saw her approach. (133) The repercussions of bearing an illegitimate child who was bestowed with Shyama's husband's name were varied, from being a social stigma to a beginning of an economic conflict with the family leading to a hostile environment around her and her son.

In the story "The Reddening Tree" the plight of the parents with young daughters who are yet not married has been depicted. The daughters are considered a burden for the fathers when they are growing young. "Munni was a heavy load on her parents! Munni's heart rose to her mouth on hearing this…She was filled with disgust for herself. She was the source of all the problems in the house. She was inauspicious." (Harnot 56) To save them from the prying eyes of society, they are pressurised to marry them off at an early age. The same emotions have been portrayed by the writer through Munni's father who now looks at his daughter not as a child but as a prospective bride. The author has described the thoughts of the Munni's father sensitively in the following lines from the story.

> His eyes fall on Munni as she lies sleeping at a little distance. She is fast asleep. Mathru watches the light of the lamp gathering on her face. A few strands of hair have fallen across her cheek. Mathru has never looked at Munni in this light. Her innocence, her nascent youth, her looks. .. are all fit to be married. It seems to him that Munni grows older with every passing moment. (Harnot 53)

However, this does not end here. Even when the girl is engaged, there are so many restrictions imposed on her and her freedom curtailed to ensure her well-being and safety. "Many constraints were now enjoined upon Munni. Dos and don'ts were enforced. Now her mother did not let her go out alone." (54) It is generally believed that a few days before the wedding, the bride is more vulnerable to black magic and witchcraft which is considered to be practiced commonly by the people of the hills. In the guise of such superstitious beliefs, the girl is not allowed to move out or play with the girls in order to avoid any kind of exposure to the outer world. At the behest of these traditional conventions, limitations are forced upon her which refrains her from carrying out regular activities which may include education and professional engagements too. In the story, Munni had been forced to stay indoors which meant that the child could neither play with her friends nor could she roam about in the surroundings for her daily recreational activities. "Amma herself took the cow and goat out to graze. She did not send Munni alone to fetch forage grass. Munni could not play with other children from the neighbourhood anymore. Amma scolded her if she insisted on going out to play." (Harnot 54)

Exploitation

Shyama's exploitation began well before her marriage, being married off while she was still in her teens and had not completed her education as well. The right to education and to choose a life partner was not granted to her, making her a young victim of forceful marriage. "But her whole life had become accursed after her wedding. Her parents didn't allow her to complete even class five. Marriage was forced upon her after she left school. She was young; perhaps a couple of months short of sixteen. (134) The man that her parents had chosen for her was a crook who couldn't sustain his own life and quite apparently was incapable of rearing a family on his own. He was uneducated, an alcoholic, and addicted to drugs, detaching himself from his familial responsibilities and losing his credibility in the process.

> The man to whom Shyama was married was almost ten years older than her. Since childhood, he had had a destructive mind. When his parents sent him to school, he spent the whole day hiding in the fields and the forest. He was useless at work. Hardly had the smell of his mother's milk left his mouth and he developed the habit of drinking and taking drugs. Evil deeds. Bad company. Lies and deceit flowed through every vein in his body. (Harnot 134)

Shyama suffered greatly at the hands of her drug-addicted husband who had become a liability for her. He robbed her of all her belongings that were sold to cater to his needs for drugs and alcohol. The disappearance of her clothes and jewelry was attributed to her by her in-laws who accused her of stealing them instead. She becomes a victim of domestic violence at the hands of her husband.

> He harassed her greatly. He beat her without reason and at times he also tore her clothes. One by one, the wedding ornaments that she had kept with such care started disappearing every week. First the earrings, then the heavy silver bracelets, and after that the silver ring and anklets, all disappeared. Then, it was the turn of the symbols of marriage–the round golden hairclip and bangles. After a few days, even her clothes began to vanish one by one. Shyama was at her wit's end. Finally, she took courage and told her mother-in-law everything. The mother-in-law told her husband. Despite being in the know, they blamed the daughter-in-law herself. They accused her, instead, of taking away the clothes and ornaments to her parents' home. (Harnot 135)

After her husband's mysterious death, she faced the stigma of being a widow who had brought bad luck to the family. She shifts to her parent's house as there was no other option for her to live anywhere else. However, the property rights are not granted to the daughter which makes her an unwanted guest in that house too. She was harassed by her sisters-in-law, and her brothers ignored the situation completely. She finally decides to return to her in-law's house. "Shyama stayed quite happily with her parents till they were alive. But after them, her misfortunes returned. The taunts of her sisters-in-law became intolerable. Her brothers too didn't care for her. (Harnot 136) In her in-law's house, many attempts were made by her in-laws to suppress her and also impede her legal property right. She was at their mercy to get the necessities like food and shelter. All the attempts were made to throw her out of the house which she resisted and managed to endure all the hardships that came her way.

> No one talked to her properly. They were aware that it was not easy to legally turn her out of the house. So, they began to trouble her in various other ways. She, however, bore their offensive behaviour stoically. She didn't lose courage and endured everything they did resolutely. In the end, they had to give Shyama a couple of fields as her share of the property. And in order to drive the burdensome woman out of their way they gave her one room in the cowshed to live. She accepted this without demur. At least, she had a roof over her head. (Harnot 136)

Shyama was not provided with enough food from her in-laws which compelled her to work as a labourer to earn a daily wage. Shyama often took credit from the local shopkeeper who was an influential man in the village who obliged her and made sure that his favours were returned by Shyama. "He never lent money without a selfish motive. Whenever he saw Shyama, he swaggered a little too much. He was insolent and even obscene with her. In need of credit, she was compelled to put up with all this." (Harnot 137). The shopkeeper Lala Dhari Singh lured Shyama further by offering her more help in the form of financial assistance provided by the government for the widows by speaking to the pradhan of the village. More benefits in money and kindness were assured to her for whom she was exploited by the Lala sexually at his behest.

> One day the lala said to Shyama that he would talk to the pradhan to grant widow pension to her and get some amount sanctioned for her to build a house. He would also help her to get a ration card so that she could get cheap and free rations. In this hope, Shyama began to go to the pradhan's house every day. After a few days, her pension came through. (Harnot 137)

She was further exploited by the pradhan whom she had contacted for getting the money sanctioned for the construction of her house. "The pradhan had taken the responsibility of constructing her house upon himself. Although, she well knew that he was devious and shrewd, what else could she do but agree? She had to get the work done somehow." (Harnot 137). The lines depict the desperate need that Shyama was in to get a house built for her and her son Manu. The hypocrisy of the temple's priest is exposed in the story narrating how he too was not left far behind in exploiting Shyama who otherwise belonged to a lower caste. The caste hierarchy and untouchability are not followed by the high-class priest who would otherwise maintain a certain distance from the lower caste. "One day the temple priest also came with the pradhan to Shyama's house. She was astonished. He bathed at least twice if he touched an outcast by chance. And here he was in the house of a Dalit widow, Shyama …?" (137) Circumstances had shown a different side of society to Shyama. The general conceptions and notions about the influential men turned out to be false and deceptive. The male hegemony was evident in every sphere of a woman's life and even a poor widow, already a victim of circumstances wasn't spared from being subjugated and exploited.

> There was evil in every heart, whether of a politician or a pradhan, a pandit or a thakur, a teacher or a patwari. What to say about her family? Relationships were only illusions or pretence. No one cared for anyone. Everyone had ulterior motives and purposes. They thrived only by exploiting the poor. And if they saw a woman, they neither feared the devata nor cared for religion; not even for caste or untouchability. Even useless decrepit old men, having many daughters and daughters-in-law, go wild with lechery once they are under the influence of liquor or cannabis. (Harnot 138)

Looking at the economic perspective of this pregnancy and the child, Shyama's property would be inherited by her son which became a cause of great concern for Shyama's relatives. "The father-in-law knew that if the child was registered in the panchayat register, he would become heir to his whole share in the property. (138) Shyama was a victim of sexual exploitation by the numerous men of her village and for the welfare and ensuring secure future for her son; she ensured that he gets an education like the other boys of her village. While filling up the details of the boy's school form, she named her dead husband as his father. "When he asked her the name of the boy's father, Shyama was embarrassed. But the very next moment, she took hold of herself and gave her husband's name. (Harnot 138). This issue was raised by Shyama's father-in-law and to decide on the matter the panchayat was called. "Her father-in-law created one more problem for her. He filed a case in the panchayat that this immoral woman had brought dishonour to their family." (139) The next story presents the exploitation of women in society at the hands of male relatives in their lives is "Daarosh". As explained in the footnote of the story, "Daarosh is a word widely spoken in a tribal area of Himachal Pradesh. It means to use force or power. The tradition of 'coerced marriage' that prevails in that particular area is called "Daarosh dublub", which means to "marry forcibly. "This is a sheer encroachment on the rights of a woman to marry the man of her choice and is rape in disguise of a traditional wedding.

> … Two young men of the tehsil, with the help of some accomplices, forcibly kidnapped a girl of the village who was going to see the tournament with her friend to a nearby school. They took her to a cave close by. Then the friend and other youngsters left. Only the one who wanted to marry her stayed on and had sex with her against her will… (Harnot 60)

The writer also throws light on the polyandry system of marriage where a woman has more than one husband and usually, they all are brothers. "They were three brothers. Only Kaanam's Bade Pita had performed the marriage rituals. However, Ma was wife to all of them." (Harnot 64) The physical and mental stress that a woman has to go through while performing her domestic duties is elaborated upon in the lines from the text. Besides the home, the ladies of the house are also responsible for looking after their agricultural and horticultural produce. They participate actively in the complete process starting from the plucking of fruits to the further processing of the fruits produced in their orchards and farms. The management of the home and hearth as well lies entirely on their shoulders.

> Kaanam was surprised to see that every evening people from other villages came home with Bade Pita. They sat drinking copiously and Ma sat until midnight to attend to them. She would have her dinner only after everybody had eaten. In addition to this, she had to satisfy two husbands. Also, she had to pluck seasonal fruits off the trees, and dry and preserve these for winters. Apricots and apples being chief among them. (Harnot 70)

The tremendous amount of work done by the ladies of the house is taken for granted by the men who presume that they are used to this way of life and have no qualms about it. For the women too, this format of working had been accepted without complaining or questioning. "Not only this, once or twice in a week Ma had also to make grape wine. But Kaanam had never seen any resentment in her eyes or a frown on her face. She had never felt that Ma was ever tired." (Harnot 71) The hypocrisy in the custom of 'Daarosh' has been depicted in the story where the girl who defies this tradition and comes back from the clutches of her kidnappers, had to live in society carrying the stigma of being raped. Had she quietly accepted her sexual abuse at the hands of the boy, she would have been living a dignified life and enjoyed the privilege of being called his wife.

> She thought to herself how strange these traditions were. If the girl had given in quietly, she would have been a wife. Now she is wasting away with the blot of rape on her. Kaanam was filled with such abhorrence for her society as if all this were happening with her. (Harnot 72)

In the story "The Reddening tree" Munni is not allowed to go to school after a certain age. Rather she has been groomed to get married and become a dutiful wife by carrying out the household chores efficiently. No wonder Munni is adept at every household chore even at her tender age. She churns milk, makes maize and wheat Rotis, fetches water and forage, milks the cattle, works the millstone, and even takes grain to be ground at the watermill. ... These ideas are fed into her mind from an early age which conditions her to be prepared for a future that is deeply embedded in the traditional values which question her identity as a child of her parents. "... a daughter is another's treasure; she should be accomplished at making a home." (Harnot 48). Munni is being trained by her parents to be adept in household activities but she misses her school. "Munni still remembers when she had stood first in class. How much love and appreciation the teachers had given her.

How many 'well dones' had come her way!. .." (Harnot 48) The right to education has been encroached upon in Munni's case and she has been denied a promising future due to the orthodox ideology followed by her family. Munni, however, still longs to go to school. But Bapu doesn't let her. He believes there is no use in schooling a girl. He allowed her to attend school till class three. Then he withdrew her name." (Harnot 48) Many girls have not been allowed to continue with their studies owing to the conventions of not allowing the girls to socialise with the children who belong to the various communities. "Ma used to remonstrate with Mathru for spoiling Munni by sending her to school at all, "There are children from all kinds of families in the school. Now our Munni will sit with low castes. Even eat with them. ..."' (Harnot 48) The casteist perspective also hurts the girls who are deprived of education due to illogical practices and orthodox beliefs that restrain them from gaining education with the children of the lower castes.

The story has depicted the plight of the young and unmarried girls of the families. The daughters are considered to be a burden on the family till the time they're married. Their marriage too is a matter of grave concern for the family, ranging from the choice of groom to the accumulation of money for performing the ceremonies. This leads to a feeling of dejection among the girls who "Munni was a heavy load on her parents! Munni's heart rose to her mouth on hearing this. She was beginning to understand the situation now." (Harnot 56) The daughter's marriage is considered to be a great deed that earns the parents' immense respect. The daughters are given away to the boy's family and this custom is called 'Kanyadan' which means donating your daughter to another family and thus equating her to some material or money that is parted with for the recipient's welfare or benefit. The girl is made to shift her home and her affiliation with her parents' family is completely changing her identity.

CHAPTER 11

Quest for a New Feminist Identity: Defying Conventions of the Society

The elements of change in the society have been portrayed by showing how the girls from the villages of the tribal areas are being sent to the cities for gaining education. These radical changes in society ensure that the lives of the girls in the hills are no longer subject to the age-old odd traditions. They now have the liberty to make the important decisions of their lives on their own without any restrictions. They could take up a career to be financially independent or marry the man their choice. "Kaanam must have been six years old when Ma, amid many pressures from the family, sent her to the city." (63) Her family thought of sending Kaaanam away to the city would prevent any kind of traditional obligations on her and allow her to lead a life free of the orthodox conventions followed in her area. Social conventions were harsh, particularly for girls which prompted her parents to ensure her well-being and safety by educating her in the city. As is evident in the lines from the text quoted below:

> Probably, there was no girl in the village more educated than Kaanam; not only in the village but in the entire region. Ma thought that she would forget everything in the city. After completing her studies, she would take up a job or marry a man of her choice. (Harnot 66)

Daarosh has long been accepted by the people as a tradition to comply with. However, the writer has narrated an incident where it has been challenged legally by the girl who was kidnapped. In a very transformative judgment, the culprits who performed this act of kidnapping a girl and marrying her against her wishes were taken as a violation of her dignity. It had now become a punishable offense and the court directed the government to take steps to create awareness and abolish this custom.

> "... The court, declaring this incident as being against the dignity of the woman and of the law, had ordered punishment for both the young men on the charge of raping the girl. This historical judgement was pronounced after having found them guilty under the Indian Penal Code

> (IPC) sections 366, 368, and 376. The one who had sexual intercourse with the girl was handed four years imprisonment along with a penalty of three thousand rupees; while his friend was sentenced to three years imprisonment and a penalty of fifteen hundred rupees. In its judgment, the court said that the tradition of kidnapping a girl and marrying her forcibly is unfortunate. This tradition, in which girls and women are humiliated and treated like animals, is a blot on society. The court asked the state government to realise the seriousness of this problem and take necessary steps to end this social evil." (61)

However, Harnot also tries to portray the mindset of the older generation who don't see the court's decision as a ray of hope for the people who have defied this tradition. The ground reality is far from the rosy and bright future that the younger generation would want to project. People have more faith in the social conventions, ignoring the intrusion of modern thoughts that would allow girls to live a dignified life by not conforming to or rejecting this prejudiced custom of male domination. "But for Kaanam's Ma, the present was no different from the past. For her, the contemporary was the same as it used to be years ago." (Harnot 63) The protagonist of the story herself becomes a target of this custom of forcible marriage, but she retaliated and didn't let her succumb to the physical domination of the boys who tried to kidnap her. Kanam vigorously retaliated against the assault attempted on her and managed to foil their plan. This incident propelled her to revert at the boys as strongly in an attempt to refrain herself from falling into their clutches. "No one knew how Kaanam managed to escape their hold. After that, the way Kaanam beat them with blows, kicks and head butts was enough to amaze anybody...Kaanam was fighting with the boys. (Harnot 73)

In the story "Slur", during the proceedings of the Panchayat, Shyama was insulted and questioned, asked to reveal the name of the child's father. Shyama gained strength and managed to name all the men who had subjected her to sexual exploitation at their behest to help her financially. The startling revelation was made when Shyama named her father-in-law whose name was taken by her so loudly that it defied all the traditions that are followed by the daughters-in-law in the society by not addressing the names of their elders. This exposure rendered everyone speechless and they could now no longer question the right to property of the widow's son. "The headmaster opened the register. He turned a few pages ...Then he shook off the excess ink and stroked out the name of the child's father. He now wrote a new name... Manu Dutt, son of Smt.

Shyama Devi." (Harnot 143). These above lines narrate an important turn in the conventions as the social norms were challenged and altered in the case of Shyama by giving her a new identity as the sole guardian of her son. She was now a single parent and a single mother to her son, taking the place of the child's father. However, this story ended humorously, subtly pointing at the mindset of the men in authority who consider her name against the father's name as a spelling mistake committed by the earlier official and change the name into a masculine one as a correction.

> After his transfer, another headmaster joined the school. When he saw the register, he had a hearty laugh at finding the father's name entered as "Smt. Shyama Devi". He swore freely at the incompetence of the former headmaster. Then very neatly, he rectified the entry in the register: Father's name – "Sh. Sham Dev." (144)

The narrative is abruptly ended here very ambiguously by the writer who tactfully brings a twist to the story. This dramatic climax puts all the confusion to rest as the whole conflict of being a single parent or not is diluted circumstantially avoiding any further elaboration on this matter. The author cleverly steers clear of any contention over the subject. The author's craft as a storyteller is evident and is commendable as well. The action of the new office clerk who changes the name is a coincidence that would never be doubted in the future and would prove to be beneficial for Shyma too. This is a sort of blessing in disguise and would lead to no further discussion or clarification at any level in the future.

Conclusion

Therefore, it can be established that the feminist identity has definitely been sought and achieved by the female protagonists in the stories in the form of a single parent, embracing nature as a life partner or resisting the traditional mode of marriage. The story of the widow Shyama raises serious questions in the male-dominated society where the woman who does not have a male member as her guardian is subject to exploitation at all levels within and outside her family. She leads a deplorable life where she has no access to the necessities of life and is at the mercy of others. To gain any kind of financial independence, she has to labour hard as a wage earner and is also used for the domestic household work by the family members. She has been sexually exploited by the influential members of the society who offer her economic assistance and also ensure to help her in the supervision of the construction work of her house which is again considered to be a man's domain. Even though widows have a right to their deceased husband's property and her father-in-law's property, Shyama had to struggle for the same. The concept of a single-parent or single mother is alien to the rural world in India and this narrative has been able to bring forth this issue very effectively. There is a need to implement the laws laid down by the government at the grass-root level by bringing awareness among the women. The education of women needs to be assured so that they are made aware of their rights, the marriage below the age of eighteen years should be checked and the employment of the widows may be ensured so that they are not subjected to exploitation at the hands of the powerful men. Similarly, "Daarosh" too emphasises the need to eradicate the social evil of forcible weddings where a woman is subject to physical assault and later married, most of the time in a planned way where the girl's parents are also party to this tradition which doesn't allow the girls to marry the man of their choice. The need to make people aware of the women's basic right to choose their husband is more important. Munni in "The Reddening Tree" has portrayed the innocence of the little girl whose tender mind finds it easier to adopt a tree as a husband rather than getting married to a boy traditionally which would force her father to sell his lands to follow the customary rituals of the society. The simple logic applied by Munni is an easy way to untangle the complexities that would arise with her marriage and deprive her father of the ancestral lands.

CHAPTER 12

Narrative on Deity Worship and Belief System in the Himalayas

This chapter attempts to explore the concept of faith and devotion towards the deities that are not only worshipped but are the driving force behind any endeavour in the village or the regions where they reside. The deity or the 'Devta' as they are referred to by the people in their native language, influence the lives of the people very strongly, being a part of their everyday lives besides being worshipped on all the festivals and auspicious occasions. Such is the belief system of the natives that the deity is consulted before taking any important decision or finalising a project or activity. The deity is blended in the environment of the hills and the faith of the people in these gods is as natural as living and breathing. Their lives are blended with the faith in the local gods that are entrenched in their minds since they gain consciousness. As Molu Ram Thakur elaborates in his book Myths, Rituals, and Beliefs in Himachal Pradesh, "They dwell in rivers and ravines, in springs and streams, in brooks and lakes, in valleys and dales, in stones and rocks, in trees and plants, in fields and high peals, over mountains and hills, in woods and forests." (Thakur 51) The deities reside in nature which is considered to be the manifestation of the gods and goddesses. He further talks about the reasons why they are thought to be mingled and merged with nature. "In fact, they live everywhere because there are Gods who are homeless and also wandering deities." (51) Such is their aura in these regions and in the daily lives of the people that any occasion is considered to be incomplete without them. "They are so closely connected with the metaphysical and religious life of the hill people that there is hardly any activity which is beyond their sphere of influence they are numerous and their deitification is highly diversified." (58)

The archetypal criticism is a way in which the deity's description in the texts can be analysed. Archetypal images are created in the text where the pattern and rituals worshipping the local gods and goddesses are region-specific and are found in the literature of hills. ".. the term archetype denotes narrative designs, patterns of action, character types, themes, and images that recur in a wide variety of works of literature, as well as in myths, dreams, and even social rituals." (Abrams 18). These denote the specific symbols and motifs in the texts that are repeated while referring to the similar customs that are followed and the rituals that are performed in the specific ceremonies in the hilly regions that are like the "... elemental patterns of myth and ritual that, he (Frazer) claimed, recur in the legends and ceremonials of diverse and far-flung cultures and religions." (Abrams18)

The idea of a deity is not region-specific to the hills of Himachal alone but is prevalent in every part of the country. The different civilisations of the world have their own set of beliefs and worship the various forms of Gods and Goddesses according to their faiths and conventions that have been formed through the ages. As PCK Prem elaborates "A cursory look at the history of folk literature of different regions and countries, despite variations in lingua franca, traditions, rituals and customs and cultural differences, conveys perennial truths in a spirit of harmony while it beautifies humanity." (12). All the religions of the world imbibe the principles and doctrines of trust in the symbols of power. God's presence was realised and felt by the people by personifying it. As is clear from these lines, "Epiphany" means "a manifestation," or "showing forth," and by Christian thinkers was used to signify a manifestation of God's presence within the created world." (Abrams 114) Initially, the fables and tales were narrated through the older generation in an oral form that formed an important constituent of the folklore. "Folklore," since the mid-nineteenth century, has been the collective name applied to sayings, verbal compositions, and social rituals that have been handed down solely, or at least primarily, by word of mouth and example rather than in written form. Folklore developed, and continues even now, in communities where few if any people can read or write." (Abrams 138) PCK Prem elaborates on folk literature: "Folk literature constitutes psychological, cultural and philosophical areas of growth and development of a country and in the background wholesome ingredients of folklores and folktales stay to reflect on a country's culture, ethos, and heritage." (Prem 8)

The Morality Plays were staged to strengthen the beliefs of the people in their religious ideologies, saints, and God. The folktale, strictly defined, is a short narrative in prose of unknown authorship which has been transmitted orally; many of these tales eventually achieve written form. (Abrams 139) The verses in the plays then took the form of prose gradually transforming them into tales. The representation of the God, deities, and saints became an important part of the prosaic literature as well of that region. "The detailed representation in the prose fiction of the setting, dialect, customs, dress, and ways of thinking and feeling which are distinctive of a particular region." (Abrams 201). In the stories of SR Harnot, the devtas bring about important twists and turns. The stories that would be dealt with the theory of faith in the local deities are "Swarna Devta Dalit Devta", "The River has Vanished", "The Saddle" and "Aabhi". In the stories, the deities are placed in a very privileged and elevated position and connected to them spiritually as well. Besides the regional affinities of the people, the devtas and devis also influence the ecological dynamics of the places that people believe are dependent on them. The human interactions with the natural environs create problems that are eventually rectified by the deities themselves according to the strong beliefs of the people. "Himachal Pradesh is a treasure trove of rich local heritage, as manifested in its traditions, art and culture. An essential aspect of this heritage is the focus on native gods (*devtas* and *devis*), which was an integral part of the belief systems of the earliest tribal groups who lived in this region" (Sharma et al). People of Himachal and their belief system has been encapsulated in the stories of Harnot who has vividly portrayed the customs and rituals associated with the worship of the local deities.

Tradition and Faith

The stories depict an immense amount of faith that people have in the deities of their villages and regions. The stories impact people psychologically who believe that devtas have been hovering around them for ages and are supremely powerful. "The devta or devi plays a central role in the community. The temple complex is the most important building, usually located at the top, or in the centre, of the village. Over time, the community grows either radially with the temple complex as the centre, or extends out below it, depending on the topography of the area." (Sharma et al) Not a single incident or event takes place in the region without the prior permission of the devta. The deity's permission is required if something is to be added or changed in the village with regard to construction, land use, services, etc. If he is displeased, his anger is expressed by some inauspicious occurrence that takes place in the region. People then try to please the deity by making offerings or by communicating with the disciples that are called 'chelas' and are believed to be possessed by the deity when invoked. It is through the 'chela's body that the deity speaks to the people. People of the regions listen to and narrate the age-old mythical tales that have been passed on for generations about the local deities and their feats that strengthened the faith of the people over them. The concept of good triumphing over evil has been depicted in these tales that also act as a lesson of morality and inspire the people to follow the virtuous path. The devil is relegated to a position that teaches people to refrain from wrong deeds.

The village festivals revolve around the worship of the deity, with the festivities usually consisting of carrying the palanquin of the devta Devi through the village or collaborating with neighbouring villages in holding small fairs that are to be an opportunity for the gods of the respective villages, as well as the village residents, to get together. Local functions and marriages are performed and celebrated only with the permission of or under explicit orders from the isht-devta (Main Deity) or kul-Devi (Goddess of the Clan). It is not only out of fear but also out of reverence and deep faith that the commands of the deity are followed and adhered to. It is believed that, in exchange, the devta or devi will protect them from harm and misfortune. The devis and devtas also protect the forests in their region of their dominion and rule. Cutting even a single tree requires their permission. The palanquins of the gods are also made of wood from these forests. In local temples, the idols are made of gold, silver, or electrum which is an alloy of silver, gold and other elements. The deities are placed on wooden palanquins and are dressed in traditional costumes and ornaments – each unique with respect to the others. Local deities are very personal to the communities that worship them. They are present in the daily lives of their devotees, guiding, commanding and counselling people, anticipating problems and helping confront them. People pray to their own deity for good health, good crops, and rain, as it is believed that these things are under the deity's control. Each devta or devi have their own customs, and they have indicated how they prefer to be worshipped. As a result, local rituals and forms of worship and prayer vary from area to area. Deities decide on the implementation of governmental and non-governmental policies in the area as well – their approval is mandatory. Most of the festivals celebrate the changing seasons and the end of harvest. Deities are asked to bless the people and protect them from misfortune. It is believed that the gods visit Heaven, or Indrapuri, during winter, and that they sleep between July (Shravan) and October (Kartik), so it is during these months that temples and palanquins are repaired and improved, and when non-religious folk festivals are held. The people of Sarain are god-fearing. To expiate guilt, for example, silver 'hands' are donated to deities, symbolising the sinner sacrificing the part of themselves that committed the sin.

> Nostalgic memories of the village, ancestors surviving in faint reminiscences, history, and ancient times continue haunting a man throughout life. He derives pleasure, shares poignant moments, and keeps empathetic treasure intact. Battles among gods and demons (suras and asuras), men and gods, gods and goddesses, glimpses of worlds and regions unknown excite men all over the world irrespective of age, religion or region. Ideas of paradise and hell, men walking on earth with supernatural powers, gods descending on earth in different incarnations and educating men to appear charismatic. Many tales stir feelings of sanctity, faith, fears of suffering and death. Battles and conquests related to men, gods, goddesses and daityas (Monsters) confound minds and here, a few mysteries grow and decline to let slip the origin for the inquisition. (Prem8-9)

The customs and rituals of the regions are followed to honour the deity during special occasions. Sometimes in the hills, a person may invite the deity to his house and the moment is celebrated with a lot of pomp and show. The procession is taken out on the path that the deity travels on to the house of the host. The occasion is marked with a lot of gaiety as most of the time the deity is called when a wish is fulfilled or some auspicious occasion has to be celebrated. "Last evening the devta had come to Leeladas Sharma's home riding on his rath, the tastefully decorated ceremonial palanquin. Two more devtas had also arrived on their raths to his house. Some time ago Leeladas had promised offerings to the devtas in return for the fulfillment of his wish." (Harnot 112) During such occasions, one disciple of the deity is possessed to communicate with the followers and the host who has organised the event in the deity's honour. As Sprya Sharma explains in her article on the devtas: "The religious processions and ceremonies must be performed with the utmost discipline. Every household must personally participate and, if they are not present, they are required to pay a fine as penalty. Festivals start with Vikram Era (Nama Samvat) and each month there are fairs scheduled, including Chatrail, Bishu, Minjar, Fag, Rakshabandhan, Guganaumi, Losar, Sarai, Diwali, Sajo, Dussehra, Faguli, Basant Panchmi, Shivratri, and Holi." (Sharma et, al)

The deity is invoked by this special person who is known as the 'chela'. The deity enters the human body of this person and the presence of the deity in the chela's body is marked by trembling and shivering. A few moments later, the 'chela' starts to talk to the people around them and expresses his displeasure or happiness talking to them. He answers all the questions and guides them in taking important decisions for their bright future. He responds by shaking his head and moving his body which is attributed to the power of the deity whose presence is difficult for the 'chela' and his body to endure both physically and mentally. The whole phenomenon is explained in the following passage from the story by the author very vividly.

> When the music reached the highest pitch, the chief goor (Disciple) of the temple on whom the shadow of the deity was supposed to descend would start shaking and shivering until his whole body was in a complete convulsion. He would give a sudden jolt to his head; his cap would tumble down and his long hair would fall on his shoulders. Music would continue at its highest pitch. The gathering would watch the goor spellbound and get convinced that the goor is now in complete possession of the deity. His eyes would become red hot and face black. The other goors would also now feel the deity's shadow descending on them and they would also start shaking and shivering like the chief goor. They held small iron chains in their hands, which they shook and struck their backs thrice or five times. It was a sign that the other deities had now entered and possessed the goors. Thus possessed, the goors would bend to the ground, screaming 'hooooooo'. Now the chief goor would bang the ground with his hands and shout 'rakkhe' for 'protection. The other goors would repeat the chief goor's words. To control and guide the ceremony five panchs (chiefs) huddled around the goors. This was the beginning of the dharmachar (ritual)which would be followed by the 'petitioners' who would come one by one to reveal their problems and seek the deities' grace. The chief goor would give a patient hearing to each one of them and console them by offering solutions. (Harnot 114)

A procession is carried out when the deity travels in a palanquin which is carried by two men. The followers walk behind the deity honouring his presence and movement. The chariot is decorated beautifully and is adorned and embellished with heavy attires and jewels. The bright and shiny clothes symbolised the aura of the deity and attract the attention of the passersby who bow their heads in supplication and fold their hands to pay obeisance to the devta. They even make offerings in kind or cash which ensures the blessings of the deity on them. The grandeur and the might of the deity can be assessed by the number of people who join in the procession and the house for celebrations. The host and the followers also provide patronage for the deity so that the traditions are carried out in the society by future generations as well. The following passage would throw more light on the occasion.

> The deities riding the chariots are only symbols of the Divine. The chariot of the chief deity, which I had left behind, was beautifully made. It was built on two long wooden poles covered with silver. The canopy of the chariot is made of gold. Inside the chariot sits the gold mask-like replica of the chief deity. His chariot is surrounded by the chariots of other deities in smaller sizes with replicas made of silver and brass. One female deity is covered with yak-hair about whom it is said that she is a monster deity and, if left uncovered, she will wreak havoc on people. Wherever her glance falls, things are burnt down. But this is all hearsay and nobody has seen this. Four canopied chariots stand in all four directions, with silver bands on all four sides! Each chariot has a silver plate on which are embossed the names of the priests and the goors as if the deities were their personal property. A huge amount of silver has been used to decorate the chariots. (Harnot 120)

The homecoming of the deity was a grand event that ensured the participation of all the villagers who were involved in one activity or the other to make it successful. The author has used natural imagery to depict how even the natural environs welcomed and paid regard to the deity when he entered the domains of the village. "By far the most important are the village gods and goddesses." (Thakur58) The fields, the sun, the birds, and the winds blowing gently conveyed their reverence for the deity in their ways which have been described by the author in the lines below.

> The devatas were about to arrive. The route through which the procession had to pass had been cleaned and cow urine had been sprinkled on it to purify it so that the devatas would not be polluted. People were waiting for the devatas. Birds… had ensconced themselves on the trees around… they sang the welcome songs as the old women sang on auspicious moments… It seemed as though the sun was standing on the last step of the ladder in order to have a glimpse of the devatas and watch them greet each other. He seemed to be sending his golden rays to convey his regards to them. The golden colour of the ripe wheat crop in the fields added a new glow to the air. A gentle breeze was blowing and the waving wheat stalks seemed to be nodding their participation in the ceremony. (Harnot 60)

The musical notes that are played for reception by the traditional pipe players also play an important role in greeting the deity. "When a devta or devi travels, a whole caravan travels along with them, including the chharidhar, the *Bhandari* (storekeeper), the *pujari* (priest), *bajantris* (musicians), and others who are assigned specific duties." (Sharma et, al) The traditional musical instrument known as the 'narsinga' (musical instrument) emits a peculiar sound that purifies the environment, infusing celestial feelings among the people who have been waiting for the deity. "Devotion to devtas and devis is a way of life for villagers…Folk dances are a spontaneous expression of the joy of life and, together with folklore and devotional music…" (Sharma et, al) The different deities connote different myths related to them which are elaborated by the author in the stories.

> The devatas' raths began to arrive. The melody of their instruments wafted in the air. The whole village came out in their welcome. The members of the committee were standing at the gate of the jatara ground. For each devata, there was a separate plate with thick sweetened rotis(bread) as prasad, incense, and garlands. The deep sound of the narsinga (musical instrument) filled the air with thrill and excitement. (Harnot 161)

Some devtas are so aggressive and powerful that holding and controlling their movement becomes a very hard task for the bearers. The weight of the chariot increases manifolds, restricting its movement and making it difficult to move forward. "They are numerous and their deitification highly diversified. There are Jamlus, Shirguls, Pals, Gahris, Nags, Dums, Thans, Sippis, Banshiras and many others" (Thakur 58) Some devtas are considered to be more powerful and are not local but are deities who have connections with the Indian epics like Mahabharata, an example of which is given by the author in the story. "Some village gods claiming greatness among the smaller deities of the area as 'great deities' i.e., Mahadeos…. Some village gods claimed their predominance by declaring themselves or by declaring by their worshippers as 'bara deo', 'mahadeo', 'Mahasu' or even 'bara mahadeo'. (Thakur 52) Mahunag is the devta who is believed to be an incarnation of Karna. To pacify this fiery deity him, special offerings are made. A special musical note is played in his honour to please him. The author mentions his chariot and the struggle that the disciples who carry him have to go through in maneuvering him.

> Just then, the eleventh devata was seen arriving.. .He is known as Mahunag, an incarnation of the Mahabharat warrior, Karna. As soon as he reached the festival ground, he grew furious and his fury was unleashed on the bearers of the rath(chariot). The rath became very heavy. The bearers began to sweat profusely. The devata made the rath carriers run around the ground. The rath moved forward and backward. It tilted down and righted itself. The carriers found it immensely difficult to keep their hold on the rath amidst the frenzied sounds of the folk instruments. The accompanying pujari tried to pacify the devata and sought his forgiveness. (Harnot 162)

In the story "Aabhi", the goddess Budhi Nagin Ma has been depicted in hibernation form during the winters. The importance of the goddess is also very relevant in the hills and they are considered to be the manifestation of power, strength, and endurance. "The cult of Devi is, also, very prominent. She is venerated under various names" (Thakur 55) It seems that the snow around the lake has forced the goddess to remain in deep slumber. It is another way of providing a hiatus from normal natural activities. The bird aabhi too is free from her work of cleaning the lake which is now frozen. This has been mentioned in the story by the author when he writes: "Aabhi again goes to Budhi Nagin Ma's doors to make her plaint but no one hears her pleas – not even Budhi Nagin Ma; it seems she too is hiding from the cold wave, deep in the inner sanctum of the temple." (176). These lines depict the manner in which the deities in the hills are closely connected to nature and the seasons. The following lines from an article in Sahapedia elaborately describe how the temples and the devtas have been held in high esteem in the villages of Himachal Pradesh would enable us to understand how the author has been influenced by these rituals and has been able to blend these images in his stories to construct plots that are so closely associated with the devta and the belief system that exists there. It is natural for the people to be influenced by the devta and also to imbibe and embrace them in all walks of their social and religious lives.

> The people of Himachal have a unique way of celebrating fairs and performing traditional rituals to mark births, deaths, harvests, or good rainfall. Dev temples, or *kothi*s are the focal point of religion and faith for the villagers. In many places, the kothis of landlords *(thakurs)* have been converted into temples. Ancient folklore often deals with stories of gods or chivalrous heroes or chieftains. The people of Himachal love festivals and participate enthusiastically in local festivals and fairs. No religious function is considered complete without the presence of the devta.

During religious occasions, people bring out the *chhari* (the stick belonging to the devta, and symbolic of his power) and it is carried by the chharidhar. When the devta is taken on jagran, or procession, or to some other religious function, the golden chhari is always carried along. When collecting money, the silver chhari is carried by the chharidhar. (Sharma et,al)

CHAPTER 13

Phenomenon of Deitification: Evaluating Skepticism, Faith and Rationality

In modern times, with the advent of technology and high-speed mediums of transport, the relevance of the belief in Devta is rendered archaic and questionable. The new generation that has grown up using electronic gadgets and surfing the internet, finds this belief system difficult to follow. The advancement in science and the developmental changes brought about by the government and the administration have relegated the position of the deity whose consent is not taken for the planning and commencement of any activity that takes place in the region. This chapter explores the balance that humans have tried to maintain between developmental projects and the belief in a deity that persists in the people who reside in remote villages. The decisions of the government have often led to the depletion of natural sources and environmental degradation. The ecological balance has been disturbed by the construction of dams that have brought about irreparable damage to the region. The people have immense faith in the gods and goddesses which is sometimes shaken by their inability in dealing with the same.

As PCK Prem has pointed out in the lines below:

> Myths and legends, many a time, refuse clear rationalisation, and yet man begins to relate lives to the ancient tales, and conceives fresh little tales with gods, men supermen and ghosts, and animals and birds playing prominent roles in reading life. With the passage of time, folk literature became a part of life. The little tales speak not only of the predicament of earthly life but also hint at a contented and glorious celestial future. (Prem 1)

This shows that logical reasoning is often ignored by the people when it comes to worshiping their deities, the fanfare and the expensive celebrations in the processions and the feast are a kind of patronage that is provided to the deities by the rich, influential, and powerful people of the village and region. The celebrations cannot be afforded by the poor people though they revere the deities as much. This is another aspect that the author has elaborated upon. There is a streak of sarcasm in the lines which hints at the disparity between the classes and how this becomes evident on occasions like these 'jataras' (religious ceremony) which refers to the travel, procession, and reception of the deity by the villagers. This ceremony has been written about descriptively by the author and quoted below to emphasise the importance of the Deity in the lives of the people.

> No doubt jataras were held almost every year but only after somebody's wish had been fulfilled. There was always a selfish reason behind these jataras: either someone had been blessed with a child or somebody was cured of a disease. Jataras were held when somebody's business had prospered or somebody's family had come out of some difficult situation. But jatara for the construction of a road or the opening of a primary school or the election victory of a candidate or party was unheard of. Moreover, organising a jatara is not everybody's cup of tea. Apart from other things, you have to make arrangements for goats for sacrifice which is an extremely costly affair; and this done, you have to invite people from your and neighbouring villages. Every rath is accompanied by thirty or forty persons who need to be looked after with special care in matters of food and clothes. And then there was the expenditure on a number of workers who were temporarily employed during the ceremony, apart from the routine pujaris and temple employees. Each village had its own temple committee and the members of these committees had to be approached for participating in the ceremony along with the rath procession of their village devata. It was really a very complex and expensive affair. (Harnot 158)

The author has also elaborated upon the existence of the deity which people believed was in the form of an important character, Som in the story "The River has Vanished". It was this character that the people regarded as an incarnation of the devta itself considering the task that he had accomplished which the villagers could have never imagined. Their village would now be on the road map of the state as the government had agreed to connect it via the road. This was an achievement for the villagers who gave the credit of convincing the government to do it to Som. The deity had probably chosen Som as a medium for this feat or was it Som who was now the devta for the.

The crowd was so overwhelmed by these announcements that for a few moments it was dumbfounded. The people simply couldn't believe their ears that they had got such a huge bounty without even asking for it. At that moment a question lit up in their minds about who was the real devata...? (Harnot 165)

The Deity, on invocation, expressed his anger and summoned the local MLA and Chief Minister but the request was politely turned down citing administrative reasons and attributing the decision to the larger issue of the development of that area. The deity's interference in such matters was also perceived and depicted as a political conspiracy to prevent the present government from taking the credit for carrying out this developmental activity. The government plays safe by citing administrative reasons and preventing any kind of dishonoring of the deity. Taking such decisions without the consent and will of the deity is an aspect that has been depicted in the story in the following lines:

> When a group of holy men invoked the deity, he was angry. The pradhan, legislator, and the chief minister bore the brunt of his anger. Talk of total destruction was in the air. It was decided that the legislator be called before the deity. An order on behalf of the deity was issued but the legislator did not appear before him. Then an order was sent to the chief minister. In a very balanced tone, the chief minister replied that he had great respect for the deity but to bring the deity in matters of development was some kind of opposition politics. People lost hope. (Harnot 172)

The deity had now adorned another role, from being the worshipped one to that of a protestor. It had assumed the role of a leader of the protesting villagers who were struggling for their existence. This deity was symbolic of the religious ethnicity of the people. People considered the deity to be supremely powerful and mighty and hoped that its presence would play a vital role in forcing the government to revoke its decision of the construction of the dam. People had not lost faith in the devta and were still very optimistic that the devta accompanying them would make a huge difference in the attitude of the government.

> By noon, the deity reached the place of protest. Accompanying the deity were innumerable people. More than a hundred were already there obstructing the work of the company. The deity and the government's police force reached the spot almost at the same time. People had the belief that now no powers that be could crush their protest. They had the deity with them and they had the deity's might with them. (Harnot 172)

The incident of the caning and shooting by the police on the protestors in the presence of the devta was undoubtedly a very disturbing incident that had shaken the faith of the people. The audacity of the policemen, who had followed the orders from their higher authorities of disengaging the protestors and preventing them from disrupting the construction work, came as a bolt from the blue for the villagers. They were shocked psychologically and wounded physically. The silence of the deity was as mysterious as it was questionable too. "The deity watched all that silently. His power was not revealed. The oracle did not speak. The assistant oracles too were silent." (Sharma173) The delusion and shock of the people on seeing their deity helpless have been elaborated upon by the author very descriptively and vividly in the following lines from the story:

> Somehow the people were pacified and then the deity was locked up in the temple. That was the limit of their faithlessness. That day several illusions had come to an end. Several beliefs had died. The deity was lying silent in the temple. He had lost all his power. Where had all his power gone? Why did he not help the people? Why had no miracle taken place? Why did the deity not show his gigantic form? Then why had the people of the village and the entire area carried his burden? ... Such questions confronted the people again and again." (Harnot 74)

The author has not ended the story here but has kept the conclusion a little ambiguous by narrating the events that happened the next day. The news of the next day is a confusing statement that doesn't specify why and how the events that took place. The policemen who had beaten up the protestors were attacked by a mob of people. This has been described as the fury of the deity who showed his power through the villagers themselves by taking multiple human forms. The villagers had become a representative of the deity's anger and had taken revenge by attacking the policemen who were making merry by consuming alcohol and non-vegetarian food. The celebration of the policemen had turned into a nightmare for them. The faith of the devta was restored in the people and more importantly for a very genuine reason. The construction of the dam was not acceptable to the devta as it would have ruined the region's ecology and the environment. In today's world, the devta's role had become one of the religious preachers, who would consider all the modern aspects and help in the progressive works that would do good to humanity. Any activity that is undertaken in the name of development but that would have a long-lasting negative impact on the people and the environment would be opposed by the devta. His might was shown at the time when the faith of the people was on the brink of being devastated timely reaction of the deity has reinstated its position in the village. The whole incident has been described in the following lines of the story by the author:

> But the next day the newspaper headlines broke the news that people who had been the victims of oppression that day had attacked intoxicated policemen and company people who were celebrating their success with meat and drink, and also that in the morning, there was no trace of them left behind. At the scene, lay only some guns, a few lathis, dozens of broken liquor bottles, goats' heads and skin, and some torn pieces of khaki uniforms. Perhaps the deity, whom the oppression of the police had turned into a deserter, appeared collectively in the villagers and the anger of the people destroyed the oppressive arm of the government. (Harnot 175)

The next story "Aabhi" depicts the faith of the bird in the goddess that is believed to be residing near the lake. The temple near the lake has been dedicated to the goddess named Budhi Nagin Mata and who is considered to be in the form of a snake. During winters, it is believed that the snake goddess goes into hibernation. It is another way of allowing the birds to take a rest as well. The rest of the year, the lake is in liquid form and is visited by many pilgrims. The twigs and leaves of the trees are picked up by the birds. However, the litter that is thrown by the visitors is something that the bird finds difficult to clean. The winter months are like a boon for the lake and its environs as no pilgrims visit ad cause any kind of pollution. The goddess is believed to cover the area with snow all the winter months to conserve the forests and keep them free from pollutants.

> Aabhi feels that Budhi Nagin Ma weaves this entire weft and warp of winter for the sole purpose of giving Aabhi rest from her labours. It is she who brings the snow. She freezes the lake and makes it like an ice rink so that for six months not even a whit of straw or twig falls into the lake. No one comes to throw litter into it. (Harnot 178)

The forest fires caused by the men who smoke in the forests have been written about in the story. An important turn takes place when the man who negligently throws the cigarette into the forest is engulfed in himself. This is considered to be done by the goddess Budhi Nagin Ma who doesn't tolerate any kind of harm done to the forest. "Budhi Nagin Ma has awakened from her slumber and watches the man bobbing in the water from behind her doors." (183) The narrative ends here amplifying the impact of the Goddess's fury caused by the negligence of the humans that causes a large environmental damage. It is only the Goddess that can rectify the misdoings of the people by the supernatural powers that the natives believe them to possess. This would not only reinstate the faith of people in the deities but also warn about the effect of dereliction their duty and responsibility towards nature that is considered to be mother and nurturer as well.

Conclusion

The stories have tried to narrate incidences where the faith and belief in the devta are depicted vividly and the customs and traditional practices of worshiping the deity have been described descriptively by the author. With the advent of technology and advancement in science, developmental activities are being carried out for the overall development of the region and the state. The analysis has depicted the challenges, that the faith and belief system of the villagers, faces at the hands of the government. The deity is not acknowledged officially by the administration but the people's sentiments are attached to it. The instances in the chapter where the deity's faith has been questioned have been quoted adequately. There are a few instances where the violators of the natural ecology have been punished appropriately in mysterious circumstances Though the situation is ambiguous yet the people believe that these incidents took place at the behest of the gods and the goddesses. This incident reinstates the faith of the deities and also ensures the conservation of the environment at the backdrop of developmental activities. Thus, balance is struck at a very delicate point where the individual mind stops analysing the situation logically when overtaken by the euphoria and revelry surrounding the celebration of the faith in the devta. The rational evaluation is influenced by the emotional and passionate persuasion of the traditional beliefs and customary rituals that the people follow in the hills.

CHAPTER 14

Conclusion: Synopsis, Objectives and Scope

Conventions are stipulated customs and traditions that have been followed in a certain manner and have assumed a canonical stature. They are contradicted and defied if they become rigid. Modernity or contemporaneity is the modern and the present way of living which is in contrast with the traditional lifestyles. Conventions are challenged by contemporaneity which may result in a conflicting situation. To follow the traditions partially and also adopt the modern lifestyles simultaneously would lead to the assimilation of both the conventions and the contemporaneity to maintain a perfectly harmonious balance. The analysis of the stories and the conclusions have established the notion of this blending and compatibility. The research work has strived to incorporate the theories and conjectures while examining and investigating the texts. Each chapter has been able to establish that balance has been struck between the traditional and the modern ways of living.

The stories are the miniature form of a bigger narrative that has been curtailed to tell a tale that may not be as descriptive but has a purpose. There may not be a limit of words but a short story, endeavours to form a narrative that expresses the thoughts of the author effectively. Some subjects may not be as vast or the writer may not like to delve into them and aims at plot-making at a smaller level and not involving many characters or dialogues. The translation studies have been very instrumental in promoting the regional and local literature which has been written in the vernacular. The beginning of translation studies and its emergence as a major theory in the literary world has enabled the readers to delve into the realms of literature of other languages. Further, the translation work carried out in India and Himachal Pradesh has enabled the world to read the region-specific narratives that depict the cultures effectively. The customs, traditions, and conventions have been followed in the hills since times immemorial. The relevance of these traditions with education and technological advancement has paved way for the developmental activities. These conventions are found in contradiction with the modern world. The balance that the people of the hills have found by the continuation of old methods and the adoption of new ways as well. This dilemma in society which is fraught between the old and the new ways has been resolved to find an equilibrium that promotes the traditional set of norms and adopts the vogues to form an all-embracing environment.

The four stories namely "Cats Talk", "Ma reads", "m.com", and "Twenty Feet Bapuji" are analysed and the empty-nest syndrome in the left-alone parents is evaluated. All the parents are old, single, and living in their ancestral homes in their villages. Chachu(uncle) is the only character in the story who lives alone in the city to earn a livelihood for himself. However, he too lives alone in the absence of his kids. The trauma of being alone takes a toll on them which has been explained descriptively. Psychoanalysis of these characters reveals how loneliness and fear of the darkness affect their mental health bringing in the feeling of gloom and depression. The only way they can survive is by depending emotionally and financially on their pets. The other aspects that have helped these parents to combat their fears are studied. These include keeping busy with pets, doing household chores, socialising with neighbours and relatives, and reading. The conclusion explains how the empty-nest syndrome that these parents suffer from is dealt with. The works of Celia Dodd are quoted in the chapter to define and comprehend the concept of this syndrome in a better way. The book *The Empty Nest* focuses on the parents in urban areas who have different lifestyles. However, this research focuses on the left-alone parents in the empty-nest parents in the rural areas of the hills. The quotes from the authors help in analysing the psychological impacts of the empty-nest syndrome on left-alone parents.

The theory of Subaltern Studies has been applied to the analysis of the stories of SR Harnot. The stories portray the subalterns and the injustice meted out to them in a very elucidating manner. The portrayal of the subjugated classes is related to the age-old professions that have been carried out traditionally through the generations. The impact of education has seen an uprising in young generations who resist the caste hierarchies and refrain from following the professions of their forefathers. The pipe-players, the weavers, and the ceremonial 'scapegoat' are what the writer has depicted in the stories "Svarna Devta Dalit Devta", "In the Name of Gods" and "The Saddle" respectively. It depicts the caste hierarchies that these professionals face at every step-in society. "The Saddle" deals with a very important issue of human sacrifice to carry out a religious custom. A subaltern is converted into a high caste brahmin only for the successful culmination of the religious practice for that duration. If alive, he is relegated to the position of his old caste after the custom is over. This hypocrisy is aptly depicted in the story. The other issues and harassment faced by the subalterns in the form of untouchability and stigmatisation are very well portrayed by the author. The second part of the chapter describes how the casteist conventions that are followed are defied by the new generation that refuses to accept the standards of the society marginalising them, making it almost impossible for them to prosper as individuals and as a community. A plethora of instances from the text depicts the gravity of the resistance posed by these young Turks, who are persistent in their efforts to change their predetermined professions. The chapter affirms the fact that society indeed has to accept the changes and allow the subjugated classes to be at par with the upper castes.

A very significant and relevant aspect of the hills namely Environmental Degeneration and its impacts on people and the ecosystems are elaborated further. This is one issue that has drawn a lot of attention owing to the damage caused to the environment due to the building of dams and the consecutive formation of lakes, the submergence of towns and villages in the waters of the lakes, loss of biodiversity, disturbance of the ecological balance, the change of the course of the river that amounts to more complexities, water pollution, noise pollution and forest fires that haunt the people of the hills. The beauty and aesthetics of the hills are unraveled and nature is illustrated intricately in the stories forming a crucial backdrop for the plots. Many lines from the texts are quoted from the stories enhancing and embellishing the imagery. The ambiance of the hills and the effects on the general atmosphere illustrated in the stories have been instrumental in the genesis of the culture of the mountains. This depiction of the beauty is also important as it forms the essence of the hills and would cause an immense amount of emotional trauma owing to any destruction caused to them due to the developmental activities. The challenges in the form of the progressive works being carried out that claim to bring prosperity to the hills are disturbing for the environment. The building of dams and the interference of human beings in the pristine environs of the forests result in many kinds of pollution which are depicted in the text. Rampant forest fires which lead to a rapid and instant depletion are another cause of concern for the environmentalists and have been addressed very soundly in the story "Aabhi". The chapter captures the balance and reaffirms the faith in the deity and the Goddess who both were believed to be behind the supernatural occurring that takes place to conserve nature. A balance between the traditions and the outcomes of modernity like dams, lakes, and religious tourism has been struck and the impacts have been curtailed appropriately for the holistic development of the region.

The next chapters depict the feminist facets that have been sketched by the author by putting forth strongly the issues of sexual exploitation in widows, single motherhood, early marriage and the complications that arise by following the traditional custom of a coerced marriage called 'Daarosh' which is a direct encroachment on the liberty of a woman. The stories that have taken up are the "Daarosh", "Slur" and "Reddening Tree". The plight of the widows in India in the story "Slur" is focused upon where the widow Shyama is stigmatised for bearing a son long after her husband's death. Her sexual exploitation at the behest of helping her by the strong men of the society has also been depicted in the stories and analysed with quotes from the text. The stories depict the harassment that Shyama has to face. In the same context, the girls who become victims of forced marriage are evaluated in the story "Daarosh" explaining the mental and physical agony that they go through. The problems faced by Munni who is not allowed to go to school and is forced to marry early are also talked about. The chapter has convincingly portrayed the defiance and intense resistance that the characters of Shyama and Kanam have been able to assert against the existing social norms. How Shyama finally gets her name for the son to be registered in school and how Kanam has successfully foiled an attempt to be abducted and be another victim of the forced marriage is the breakthrough twist in the story that establishes these characters as the crusaders of women's rights.

The later chapters venture into the realms of the unique practices of the worship of the local deities and the endeavours to represent the faith, conviction and dependence of the people of the hills on these gods and goddesses. It is aimed at looking into the relevance of the deities in the present cybernated and digital world where these age-old practices seem archaic. It strives to delineate the peculiar and idiosyncratic ways of venerating and revering the deity in the traditional mode without any alterations. The chapter exhibits the faith and belief that the people of the hills have in the deity in the stories "Svarna devta Dalit Devta", "The River Has Vanished" and "Aabhi". The interrelation and interdependence of nature and the deities are very well described in the stories and have been appropriately conveyed in the chapter as well. This research aims to bring to the fore the indigenous religious practices of the people of the hills for whom the deities are an indispensable part of their lives. The challenges faced by the belief system are elaborated. The advent of modernity has been able to puncture the credence of the religious sanctity that people have placed on the deities. They beseeched on the deity with complete supplication without doubting or questioning, however, the events in the story led to circumstances where the people's faith was shaken and shattered. The dilemma and predicament that the people went through were important to be depicted in the story which the author has done remarkably in a very sensitive and tactful manner. However, the euphoric celebration of faith during festivals leads to an unquestioning stance toward the deity by the modern and educated youth that relegates logical reasoning to the margins. The reinstatement and reaffirmation of the faith in the supreme power deity are instrumental in the reinstitution and reinstalling of the deity's divine position in society. The chapter further depicts the balance that the traditional deity worship helps in maintaining to conserve the environment which is fraught with the negative impacts of human intrusion in the wilderness and man's interference in the ecosystems of the regions.

Findings

- The 'left behind, empty-nested elderly parents' of the out-migrated children adjusted to the new life by adapting to the modern and traditional methods of leading an economically and emotionally independent life.
- The women characters have assumed control and resisted patriarchal rules by taking important decisions like marriage and being a single parent, rejecting the social norms, and ignoring the taboos, asserting the new identity of women.

- Education has helped the subalterns to understand the dynamics of the casteist milieu of the society and encouraged them to deconstruct the hierarchy by manipulating the rules of casteism in their favour. Instead of being exploited, they have utilised their newly acquired status for their welfare, elaborated with depiction and resistance.
- The cultural heritage has been disturbed by the modern lifestyles of people but they have still managed to keep them alive simultaneously in context with the role of the deity in conserving the environment.

Scope for Further Research

Though the major concepts have been covered extensively in this book, however, there is still ample scope for further exploration in the stories of SR Harnot in *Cats Talk*. The themes that have been taken up in this particular research pertain to important and relevant topics, there are many more areas that need to be analysed and written about. The theme is eco-feminism in "The Reddening Tree" is one theory that can be explored and written about descriptively. The deity worship in the hills and the customs that are followed is another concept that needs attention and intense study. This particular theme would help in evaluating the local belief systems keenly and thoroughly juxtaposing them with the daily lifestyles of the people, celebrations of special occasions, and religious ceremonies. The deity and its manifestations in the different villages across the mountainous region is a subject that requires deep analysis and needs to be evaluated anthropologically along with the historical chronology and its impact on the people and the literature of the state. The phenomenon of the deity's entering into the body of the goor(disciple) is an interesting feature that needs to be evaluated. The psychological impacts of the deity's presence on the goor and the people around would make an interesting study.

Environmental degradation has been depicted by SR Harnot in the stories and this issue needs further exploration in context to the livelihood of the people. The impacts of the dams on the traditional methods of farming and grinding have also been talked about which can be analysed comprehensively. Other than the environment, the man-animal relationship is another aspect that has been depicted descriptively in the stories and can be looked deeply into. The cats, dogs, goats, horses, birds, and the milch cattle reared by the natives are a source of income and also provide emotional assistance for the people of the hills. They are important assets for the people who thrive on them for their livelihood.

The texts can be analysed using the Marxist point of view by looking deeply into the social and economic hierarchies that exist in the social structure and which are not based on caste alone. The higher caste brahmin has become poor and is a victim of the professional rivalry that exists within his community. He had to mortgage his lands and meet the expenses of his family which is a fine example of the trap that poor people fall into which is very well depicted in the story "The Reddening Tree". In other stories, the traditional landowners have been depicted as the aristocratic and noble class of the villages in the hills who don't wish to give up on their lavish lifestyles and consider the downtrodden as their inferiors regardless of the education and the employment that these people have gained long after feudalism was abolished. Economically too this elite class has been still been earning from the lands that they have inherited from their forefathers, leaving them dynastically rich.

The political scenario of the hills and the role of administration in decision-making and implementation of policies is another aspect of the stories which has been put forward emphatically. The stories "The River has Vanished", "The Saddle" and "Daarosh" have depicted the political and administrative power that demonstrates responsibility that lies in the legislature and the executive branches of government. Decisions like the building of dams and the performing of religious ceremonies are patronised by the officials as depicted in the stories. This may be explored as a topic for further research. The casteist aspect has been analysed, in context to the traditional professions followed by a particular caste through the generations and how education has affected the new generation, in this thesis. The caste hierarchies that exist in the society in the form of separate housing settlements and paths can be compared to the hierarchies depicted in the literature of the other states and regions where the same practices are found.

Contribution to Research

The research has categorically imbibed the contrasting features of the organic and the recent social norms which co-exist in the mountains owing to the rugged terrain which has yet not been invaded and influenced by the ultra-modern lifestyles. The prerequisites for adopting such a behavioral pattern don't exist in the hills which forms an obstacle for the people. Traditional methods are still clung to as the proximity to nature makes it necessary and inexorable for the people to follow them. The chapters aim at proving that the author SR Harnot has portrayed the dilemma of the people who swing and sway between the conflicting models of society. It could motivate the scholars to take up the literature of their regions and areas as a topic for further research. The translation of the texts into the native languages is very important for enabling them a wider readership. The analysis attempts to be a comprehensive one to encompass all the important and relevant aspects covered in the stories. They are evaluated from the perspective of the major critical theories of literary criticism. It would help the scholars who want to study the regional literature to understand and delve into the dynamics of social life and also formulate an organised research plan for more literary works of the writers of Himachal Pradesh.

Bibliography

Primary Sources

Harnot, S.R. *Cats Talk*. Edited by Meenakshi F. Paul and Khem Raj Sharma. Cambridge Scholars Publishing, 2018.

.... *Daarosh Tatha Anya Khaniyan*. Aadhar Publication, 2001.

.... *Jeenkathi Tatha Anya Kahaniyan*, Panchkula, 2008.

.... *Litton Block Gir Raha Hai*, Aadhar Publication, 2014.

.... *Panja*, Lalit Parkashan, 1987.

Secondary Sources

Abrams, M. H. *A Glossary of Literary Terms*. Cengage Learning, 2012.

Ambedkar, B.R. "Castes in India: Their Mechanism, Genesis and Development", *Indian Antiquary,* vol XLI, 1917.

.... *The Untouchables: Who Were They and Why They Became Untouchable*. Dr. Ambedkar Foundation, 2014.

.... *The Annihilation of Caste*, Columbia University Center for New Media, 2014.

Appignanesi, Richard, Garratt, Chris. *Postmodernism for Beginners*. Icon Books. 1995

Balokhra, J.M. *Wonderland Himachal Pradesh*. HG Publications, 1995.

Benjamin, Walter. "The Task of the Translator." *Illuminations,* Schoken Books, 1968, pp. 69-82.

Buell, Lawrence. *The Environmental Imagination: Thoreau, Nature Writing, and the Formation of American Culture*, Harvard University Press, 1995.

Clark, Timothy. *The Cambridge Introduction to Literature and the Environment*, Cambridge University Press, 2011.

Chettri, Kushmeeta, Rout, S.K. "Reading Habits – An Overview", *IOSR Journal Of Humanities and Social Science (IOSR-JHSS),* vol. 14, no. 6, pp. 13-17.

Chitre, Dilip. "Life on the Bridge" *The Bombay Literary Review,* vol.1, pp. 12, 1989.

Cheryll Glotfelty, and Harold From. *The Ecocriticism Reader: Landmarks in Literary Ecology*. University of Georgia Press, 1996.

Chatterjee, P. "After Subaltern Studies." *Economic and Political Weekly*. pp. 44-49.

Chakrabarty, Chandika. "Subaltern Studies, Bollywood and Lagaan." *Economic and Political Weekly*, vol. 38, no. 19, pp. 1879–1884.

Clark, Timothy. *The Cambridge Introduction to Literature and the Environment*, Cambridge University Press, 2011.

Devy, D.N. "Indian Literature in English Translation: An Introduction", *The Journal of Commonwealth Literature.* vol. 28 no. 1, pp-123-138.

Dodd, Celia. The Empty Nest. Hachette Digital, 2011.

.... "Fathers", The Empty Nest, Great Piatkus, 2011

Dhar, Leela. "Nature-Women Proximity: An eco-feminist reading of SR Harnot's The Reddening Tree"-*Labyrinth: An International Refereed Journal of Postmodern Studies*, vol. 10 no. 2, 2019, pp. 160-170.

Devi, Mahasweta. "Mother of 1084", *The Breast Stories,* Seagull Books*, 1997.*

Derrida, Jacques. "Des tours de Babel", *Difference in Translation.* Cornell University Press, 1985. pp. 165-207

Erickson, Roberta. "Companion Animals and the Elderly." *Geriatric Nursing,* Vol. 6, No. 2, 1985.

Glotfelty, Cheryll, Harold Fromm, *The Ecocriticism Reader: Landmarks in Literary Ecology,* University of Georgia Press, 1996.

Guha, Ranajit "The Subaltern Identity" *Subaltern Studies,* Oxford University Press.

Garrard, Greg. *The Oxford Handbook of Ecocriticism.* Oxford University Press, 2014.

Gautam, S. *Hinduism in Himachal Pradesh.* University of Oxford, 2016.

Garrard, Greg. *Ecocriticism.* Routledge, 2012

.... *The Oxford Handbook of Ecocriticism.* Oxford University Press, 2014.

Galanaki, Evangelia P. "The Origin of Solitude: Psychoanalytical Perspectives." *The Handbook of Solitude: Psychological Perspectives on Social Isolation, Social Withdrawal, and Being Alone,* edited by Robert J. Coplan et al., 2014, pp. 72-89.

Gazetteer of the Shimla Hill States, B.R. Publishing Corporation, 2012

Geertz, Clifford. *The Interpretation of Cultures: Selected Essays.* Basic Books, Inc., Publishers, 1973.

George, K.M. *Comparative Indian Literature.* Kerala Sahitya Akademi, 1984.

Giddens, Anthony (1991). Modernity and Self-identity: Self and Society in the Late Modern Age. Stanford University Press. 1991.

Glotfelty, Cheryll, and Harold, Fromm. "Revaluing Nature: Toward an Ecological Criticism." *The Ecocriticism Reader*, University of Georgia Press, 1996, pp. 225–240

Gulia, K.S. Politics and Women Empowerment in the Himalayan State. Isha Books, 2007.

Hilhorst, Lockey, Speight. "A Society of Reader." https://demos.co.uk/project/society-of-readers/October 2018.

Joshi, P.C., "The Subaltern in Indian Literature: Some Reflections on Premchand and His *Godaan.*" *Indian Literature*, Sahitya Akademi, vol. 49, no. 2, pp. 101-118.

Kumar, Pramod. "Significance of Nature and Ecocriticism in Indian Fiction in English Literature." *Pune Research Scholar*, vol. 3, no. 3. 2017.

Kumar, Sanjiv.Bhadury, Prakash. "The Marginalised Groups in Indian Social Construct: A Critical Study of Mahesh Dattani." *American International Journal of Research in Humanities, Arts and Social Sciences.* 2014. pp. 109-114.

Kumari, Shikha. "Ecocriticism in Indian Fiction." *Indian Review of World Literature in English,* vol.7, no.1, pp. 1-11.

Kumari, Shikha. "Ecocriticism in Indian Fiction." *Indian Review of World Literature in English,* vol.7 no.1

Love, Glen. Editors: Cheryll Glotfelty and Harold Fromm. "Revaluating Nature: Toward an Ecological Criticism". *The Ecocriticism Reader: Landmarks in Literary Ecology.* University of Georgia Press, 1996, pp-225-240.

Laughey, Dan. *Key Themes in Media Theory.* McGraw Hill Publication, 2007.

Meeker, Joseph. *The Comedy of Survival: Studies in Literary Ecology.* Scribner's, 1972.

Niswade, Jyoti. "Social Neglect and Oppression of Widows in Rural India: Need for Social, Economic and Policy Implication." *Enabling Gender Equality: Future Generations of Global World (Research in Political Sociology,* vol. 23.pp. 113-131.

Mcmaster University. *Reading to Escape Isolation.* Mcmasteroptimalaging.org.25 March 2020.

Mishra, Kumar Nitesh. "The Voice of Subalterns in the Novels of Aravind Adiga's *The White Tiger* and Arundhati Roy's, *The God of Small Things.*" *Impact: International Journal of Research in Humanities, Arts, and Literature.*vol.8. October 2020.

Munshi, Premchand. *Godan*, Maple Press, 2014.

Pandey, Gyanendra. "The Subaltern as Subaltern Citizen." *Economic and political weekly,* vol. 41, no. 46, Nov. 2006, pp. 4735-4741

Pathak, Bindeshwar, and Satyendra Tripathi. *Widows in India: A Study of Varanasi and Vrindavan.* Rawat Books, 2016.

Phillips, Dana. *The Truth of Ecology: Nature, Culture, and Literature in America.* Oxford University Press, 2003.

Pickering, Michael. *Research Methods for Cultural Studies.* Rawat Publication.2008.

Prem, PCK. *Folk Tales from Himachal,* Authorspress, 2017.

Quadri, Syed Mohammad. *The Craft of Language and Literary Research.* Atlantic Publishers and Distributors, 2019.

Ranjan, R. "Remembering Mahasweta Devi: A Saga of Writing on Subalterns." *Talking Humanities.* 2017. pp. 1-11.

Sharma, Vidyasagar "Subalterns in Indian Literature: Changing Narrative." *International Journal of Creative Research Thoughts,* vol. 8, 2020.

Sinha, M.P. *Research Methods in English.* Atlantic Publishers and Distributors, 2004.

Thakur, M.R. *Myths, Rituals and Beliefs in Himachal Pradesh.* Indus Publishing.1997.

Tolstoy, Leo. "Kholstomir." *The Greatest Short Stories of Leo Tolstoy.* Fingerprint Classics, 2021.

Vanashree. "Struggling Peasantry in Literary Narratives." *Indian Literature*, vol.. 29 no. 4. pp.182-200.

Valmiki, Omprakash. *Joothan: An Untouchable' Life*. Translated by Arun Prabha Mukherjee, Columbia University Press.2003

Varma, Pooja. "Abuse against Widowhood in India". *The International Journal of Indian Psychology,* v ol.4, no 1, pp. 131-146.

Internet Sources

http://epgp.inflibnet.ac.in/epgpdata/uploads/epgp_content/S000456WS/P000853/M032183/ET/1547810478Quadrant-1-widows.pdf

https://doi.org/10.1163/24685631-12340078

http://www.jstor.org/stable/4403278?origin=JSTOR-pdf

Dixon, Emeli.*https://www.bustle.com/p/does-reading-help-with-loneliness-a-new-report-says-it-could-be-a-solution-to-chronic-*

https://www.allresearchjournal.com/archives/2020/vol6issue9/PartF/6-9-163-133.pdf

https://doi.org/10.1163/24685631-12340078

epgp.inflibnet.ac.in.

https://www.jstor.org/stable/10.2307/26791383

https://www.jstor.org/stable/j.ctt1ckpcz7.15

https://www.sahapedia.org/the-tradition-and-culture-of-devi-devta-worship-himachal-pradesh. July, 2018.

https://en.wikipedia.org/wiki/Modernity

https://en.wikipedia.org/wiki/Convention_(norm)

https://en.wikipedia.org/wiki/Modernity#CITEREFLaughey2007

Index

I

L

M

N

P

R

S

T

V

W

Y